Weakfish

Bullying Through the Eyes of a Child

Weakfish – Bullying Through the Eyes of a Child

©2003, 2006 by Michael Dorn

Michael Dorn

Safe Havens International, Inc.

www.safehavensinternational.org
www.weakfish.org

ISBN 0-9741240-8-7

LCCN 2003092929

Book and cover design by Pamela Terry, Opus 1 Design
Illustrations by Barry L. Richards

Printed in Canada

Second Edition

First Printing, Hardcover, December 2005

10 9 8 7 6 5 4 3 2 1

Dedication

This book is dedicated to the many "weakfish" in our society, those children who are bullied, teased, tormented, sexually molested, otherwise criminally victimized and even occasionally murdered. May the survivors have the strength they need to carry on and to seek out advocates for the children who are in your community, waiting to lend a helping hand. My heart goes out to the families of those who have lost their lives due to the actions of bullies.

Disclaimer

The information presented in this book is designed to provide general background for the creation of a safe school climate. Readers should be aware that school and youth service professionals should seek the advice of competent legal counsel and local public safety, risk management, and emergency management personnel prior to implementing any new programs or techniques, especially those that might have legal or safety implications. Methods of implementing procedures, programs and strategies outlined in this book are obviously beyond the control of the author. Therefore, the author and Safe Havens International Inc. assumes no liability for the application of any concepts described in this book.

Contents

Dedication — v

Disclaimer — vi

Acknowledgments — viii

Introduction — xi

Forward — xv

About the Author — xviii

Preface — xvix

Stephen — 31

A Change of Scenery — 35

Respite — 43

Small People, Big Difference — 47

Back Into the Fire — 51

The Barracuda — 55

Moving Up — 73

Rebellion — 77

High School Hell — 85

Keeping up Appearances — 87

Reflections — 91

Advocates — 95

Outcomes — 101

Making a Difference — 107

Epilogue — 111

Practical Solutions — 115

Index — 167

Heartfelt Gratitude — 181

Acknowledgments

I would first like to express my gratitude to Sonayia N. Shepherd for her inspiration, kindness and support while I worked on this book. It was Sonayia who first suggested that I tell the story of a young man named Stephen as a means of helping people understand better the full impact of bullying. When I began delivering the presentation around the country, the response was overwhelming. At the suggestion of educators, mental health professionals, school resource officers and others who heard the presentation, I decided to turn the presentation into a book. Sonayia's encouragement and support continued through the time she spent proofreading and making suggestions to improve the manuscript. Her encouragement not only made this book possible, but also certainly made it far more readable and powerful than the original draft.

I would like to thank my son Chris Dorn for the role he has played in the general development of my passion for protecting children, and in particular, for the production of *Weakfish*. The fact that he matured into such a fine young man, graduating from high school and was preparing to move on to college, happened to coincide neatly with the decision to turn my Weakfish presentation into a book. His being a nearly maintenance-free son at that time contributed toward my being able to focus on writing the original manuscript and bringing the final version to print. His amazing accomplishments by the age of 18 serve as an inspiration to me. Having a teenaged son who trained thousands of educators, police officers and other government officials in 20 states; coauthored two books; had been featured on *Good Morning America, Larry King Live, ABC World News Tonight with Peter Jennings* and The

Acknowledgments

Sally Jesse Raphael Show; and appeared in an internationally utilized training video before graduating from high school would make any father proud. Seeing my son's deep concern for others and his desire to help mankind gives me even more pride as a father.

I would be remiss if I did not mention my dear friend Monique Pierson from the Garrett Metal Detector Company. Monique has been so helpful in supporting me through some very tough times and in encouraging me to work on projects like this book. Her steadfast support, as well as the time she spent reviewing and critiquing the manuscript, have been instrumental.

Similarly, Beth Richardson has been a kind and compassionate friend over the years and more than anything, has been willing to listen when it was most important.

Dr. Martha Jones has always been kind enough to take the time from her busy professional and personal life to proofread my manuscripts. Now, for the fifteenth time, she has kindly done so again. Being a true master of the English language and a lover of words makes her contribution to this project nothing short of crucial.

Jane Swift must be commended for her diligent and meticulous proofreading of the second and, later, the final draft of the manuscript, which, as with everything she has ever reviewed for me, improved dramatically from her observations.

Cindy Barber, President of the Georgia Association of School Psychologists was also kind enough to devote time from her busy schedule to review the manuscript and suggest ways to improve it.

A plethora of talented editors have also been a major influence on my ability to write with some sense of clarity and purpose. Jerry

Acknowledgments

Enderle and Deborah Moore from *School Planning and Management*, Ellen Kollie from *College Planning and Management*, Mary Noschang from *Today's School*, Tom Nelson from *Campus Safety Journal* and Caroline Ryan from *Maintaining Safe Schools* have been instrumental in my development as a writer as they worked with hundreds of very rough drafts of my articles and monthly columns. My book editors M. L. Dantzker from Prentice Hall; Hal Dawson from Ram Publishing, and Maria Nethercott, Steve LaRue and Robert Bouyea from LRP Publications have been kind, generous and patient wordsmiths. Jim Gardner, Publication Manager, and Judy Marks, Associate Director, and Bill Brenner from the National Clearinghouse for Educational Facilities have been both kind and supportive in their efforts to encourage me to write in a different style to impact architects, school planners and others through NCEF publications.

Introduction

When we released *Weakfish – Bullying Through the Eyes of a Child* a little more than a year ago, we had no idea the book would create nothing short of a movement. With three printings in the first year, *Weakfish* has generated a great deal of interest, especially as it was released with almost no marketing effort. The Alabama Department of Education provided a copy of the book to every school in the state to coincide with two state wide conferences where the author presented *Weakfish* live. Each school was provided a PowerPoint™ presentation based upon the book, and each school also picked two staff members to read the book and make a presentation of it to the rest of the school. A series of three statewide bullying prevention seminars was presented by Michael Dorn for the Council of Leaders in Alabama Schools in early 2005

The North Carolina Department of Public Instruction followed suit with a bulk order of the book, and a keynote by the author at its annual school safety conference. The presentation was equally well received at the Indiana School Safety Specialists Academy where each attendee received a copy of the book, thanks to the Indiana Department of Education. Both states included *Weakfish* as a supportive measure when their legislatures passed new anti-bullying legislation. The Massachusetts Emergency Management Agency and the Massachusetts Department of Education likewise had the author present at three state wide conferences that were well attended, despite being held during a debilitating blizzard. The state of Massachusetts has already scheduled a repeat for three more conferences in October 2005.

A few weeks later, at the Texas Safe and Drug–Free Schools Conference in Dallas, the author was interrupted four times by applause and received a rousing standing ovation while delivering *Weakfish* to a packed house of more than 1,000 attendees. Working closely with many school districts in Texas to address these issues has also been rewarding. Through the exceptional grant writing talents of Sonayia Shepherd and Russell Bentley, Safe Havens International has been able to obtain more than $3 million in U.S. Department of Education grant funding for client districts last year. These precious funds have helped our clients more thoroughly address school safety issues.

Weakfish has been presented live at more than 100 regional, state, national and international conferences across the United States, and the response has been overwhelming. A principal from Nevada, a school resource officer from Florida and a school security officer from Alabama each independently told the author that they were so moved by the presentation that they decided to forestall retirement and continue to serve as advocates for the children, and this is representative of the powerful responses from dedicated advocates we sometimes see across the country. The author has been deeply touched by countless devoted advocates for the children, like Claire Appling, who has been an educator in Brockton, Massachusetts for fifty-one years and still cared enough for the children she works with to brave three feet of snow to hear *Weakfish*. Thousands of teachers, bus drivers, students, parents, school mental health professionals, emergency management personnel, police and firefighters have listened to *Weakfish* alongside mayors, school superintendents, school board members and other elected and appointed policy makers. Attendees have repeatedly asked if the presentation was available on video format so they could share it with the staff at their schools. Hundreds of thousands more will now be able to see the presentation through the release of our new DVD, which will include my son's incredible weapons concealment demonstration, in which he produces more than 100 handguns, rifles, swords, knives and other weapons that he has concealed in ordinary clothing.

The intense and positive reaction to *Weakfish* has led us to release this second edition, which includes a number of new resources as suggested by our excellent reader feedback. These include: sample bullying survey instruments; a resource guide; suggestions for students, parents and educators for dealing with bullying situations; and a bullying reduction site survey instrument for schools from the bullying prevention program that was developed for the state of Alabama. This instrument can be used to help identify problem locations where bullying is likely to occur. When combined with surveys of students, staff and parents, it can provide a much clearer assessment of the extent and location of bullying in a school. In keeping with the Safe Havens International philosophy of teaching our clients to internalize school safety expertise rather than relying upon expensive and often unqualified private consultants, these tools are designed for schools with limited fiscal resources to address bullying.

We have also designed a set of detailed and comprehensive safe school development planning templates that help schools develop their own four-phase all-hazards school safety plans in keeping with the new U.S. Department of Education best practices model. These templates revolutionize the safe school planning process by reducing the time required for plan development by 75 to 80 percent while dramatically reducing the cost to a fraction of what school safety consultants have been charging school districts. Many of these poorly written and expensive plans purchased by districts fail to incorporate prevention and mitigation efforts focused on bullying. A free electronic copy of our complete 20-page tactical site survey instrument and sample plan templates can be found on our Web site at *www.weakfish.org/resources.html*. The site also includes a free photo tutorial that shows common characteristics within schools that make it easier for bullying to occur. School officials will be able to identify problem areas in their schools by using the Safe Havens Bullying Site Survey.

We are pleased at Safe Havens to have been able to keep salary and benefits expenses for our staff to around 10 percent of total revenues for our center during the first year of the distribution of *Weakfish*. This has allowed us to offer a variety of pro bono services to school officials and has provided the funding needed to revise the book, produce the Weakfish DVD and to publish our new book *Innocent Targets – When Terrorism Comes to School*, accompanied by an international book and bullying prevention campaign. Thanks to the support of our readers, we can continue the efforts of our nonprofit center to combat bullying and to support its victims. We hope you find this book to be helpful in your efforts to make the world a better place for children, and we thank you from the bottom of our hearts for your interest in this timely and critical topic.

Forward

Bullying does not discriminate. It is truly an equal-opportunity problem that occurs with alarming frequency on our nation's campuses. Bullying, taunting, intimidation and hazing can be found in well-funded, newly constructed suburban schools as often as they are found on inner-city campuses surrounded by blight. They occur at rural community colleges, as well as within the ivy-covered walls of America's most prestigious institutions of higher learning.

Like MTV, instant messaging and study hall, bullying is part of daily life for many children and young adults. The National Education Association estimates that 160,000 students stay home from school each day because of fear of bullies. Nearly one-third of U.S. school children said they were involved in bullying—either as the bully or the victim—at least once a week, according to a 2001 study of 15,000 young students who represented a cross section of ethnic groups and urban and rural populations.

The impact of this kid-versus-kid harassment rears its ugly head in many ways. Physical injuries are common, but, with the exception of infrequent cases of extreme bullying-related violence, these wounds usually heal. Psychological scars can fester for years. For victims, this emotional trauma often is far more than a simple loss of innocence. *Weakfish* graphically illustrates how a regular victim of bullying suffers from anxiety, depression, withdrawal and loss of esteem. This is true not just for the protagonist of this book, but for bright young students everywhere. Many are running scared every day, and in some cases, the days turn into months or even years. A Swedish study of 900 boys tracked targets of bullies into their early 20s and found that most had shed signs of heightened stress or anxiety. However, even into their adulthood, they were more likely to suffer from low self-esteem or end up depressed than those who were not bullied.

Long-term effects are not limited to the victims, either. The authors of a U.S. survey published in 2001 by the *Journal of the American Medical Association* concluded that bullying is not only a sign of troubled youth, but also can portend violence later in life.

The bottom line is that bullying occurs more than we'd like to admit, with consequences that endure for years. What can be done to stop it? Michael Dorn has filled the pages that follow with tips, ideas and suggestions that can curb bullying. Among the most important is recognizing the problem. A study by researchers at Stephen F. Austin State University found that 75 percent of students observed some type of bullying at their schools, but rarely told a teacher or an administrator. Sadly, but perhaps not surprisingly to those familiar with the problem, many students said they did not perceive teachers or administrators as interested in trying to stop bullying from occurring.

Another important step is to promote a safe school climate. Students should be encouraged to buy into the concept that a safe school means that everyone on campus is safe from guns, safe from drugs and safe from bullies. This concept of safety should be promoted universally among students, who should be encouraged to demonstrate respect (not just toward adults but toward their peers) and urged to become involved.

It is clear that Michael Dorn's years of experience as a campus safety professional make him uniquely qualified to explore the issue of bullying. In addition to his expert opinion (backed by solid research), Dorn puts a human face on the problem by telling you the story of Stephen. I hope you too will recognize this book for what it is—a call to action. For it is no longer enough to hope that humankind's capacity for goodwill can prevail on our campuses. We must all be moved to act, whether we are parents, teachers, administrators or, most important of all, students. Your active participation is the most important ingredient in making campuses safe for everyone.

Tom Nelson
Editor and Publisher
Campus Safety Journal
www.campusjournal.com
December 2002

About the Author

When the world's premier consulting firm sought the top international school safety expert, they selected Michael Dorn. Michael is the Senior Consultant for Public Safety and Emergency Management, Jane's Consultancy. Working under a unique contract with a team of top school safety experts through Jane's offices in nine countries, Michael relentlessly pursues his passion for making schools safer. Globally recognized with over 105 years of experience, Jane's is widely regarded as the world's leading provider of defense, security, and recently, school safety information. Michael also serves as the Executive Director of Safe Havens International Inc., a non profit school safety center dedicated to the development of practical and effective methodologies to make schools safe and effective learning environments.

A highly credentialed, experienced, respected and trusted expert in his field, he served with the Mercer University Police Department for 10 years before being appointed as a school district police chief. During his 10-year tenure as police chief, his department was featured as a model program by many organizations including the United States Department of Justice and the United States Department of Education. In 1999, he was appointed School Safety Specialist for the nation's largest state government school safety center – the School Safety Project of the Georgia Emergency Management Agency – Office of the Governor (GEMA). After the horrendous events of September 11th, 2001, GEMA was designated part of the Georgia Office of Homeland Security and Michael was selected as the State Antiterrorism Planner. In the spring of 2003, Michael was designated as the Lead Program Manager for the Terrorism Emergency Response and Preparedness Division of GEMA.

Michael has authored and coauthored 20 books on school safety including *Innocent Targets – When Terrorism Comes to School* and *Jane's Safe Schools Planning Guide for All Hazards* – the most comprehensive book on school safety available. He writes columns for *Campus Safety Journal, School Planning and Management, Today's School, School Transportation News* and *College Planning and Management* magazines. His training videos are now used in more than 20 countries and he has been frequently interviewed by major news organizations including *Good Morning America, Tokyo Broadcasting, The New York Times, Associated Press* and *United Press International.*

He has a Bachelor of Arts degree and a Master's degree from Mercer University and is a graduate of the 181st session of the FBI National Academy. He was selected for a fellowship with Georgia State University to train in Israel through the Georgia International Law Enforcement Exchange Program (GILEE) where he received advanced antiterrorism and counterterrorism training from the Israel Police, Israel Defense Forces and the Mossad.

Michael has served on numerous government task forces, expert working groups, and fact–finding committees. The multi-disciplinary threat management and home search techniques developed by the author and his colleagues have been used to successfully thwart numerous planned school shootings and bombings. Michael is also a powerful and popular keynote presenter and conducts intensive and advanced training sessions and consultations for school districts and private schools around the globe.

To order copies of this book, visit *www.weakfish.org*

Quantity discounts are available.

For more information on Safe Havens International visit *www.safehavensinternational.org*

About the Editor

Tricia Mosser currently edits several national newsletters on K-12 education. She is working on a master of arts in education with an elementary specialization through the University of Phoenix. She is a graduate of the University of Missouri School of Journalism. Her previous book editing projects include *Let None Learn in Fear* by Michael Dorn (forthcoming) and *The Enemy Among Us: POWs in Missouri During World War II* by David Fiedler, winner of the Missouri Governor's Award for the Humanities. She recently created www.Change-Your-World.com, a Web site with free resources for students, parents and teachers focused on encouraging young people to use their talents to help others. She can be contacted via Safe Havens International Inc. or send e-mail to tricia@change-your-world.com.

Reviewers' Observations

In order to make *Weakfish* the most powerful, motivational and effective learning experience possible for the reader, the following distinguished reviewers provided feedback to improve the book before endorsing it:

"*Weakfish* has helped me to better understand the types of situations that can, if ignored, lead to possible disaster. I will certainly pay closer attention to what is going on in the lives of children that I know."

Jerry Enderle, Editor
School Planning and Management Magazine
Dayton, Ohio

"*Weakfish* is an excellent analysis of bullying and intimidation that is frequently occurring in programs that are supposed to be protecting youth. The "chains-of-events" in the lives of youth impact their lives both in positive and negative ways, with tragic outcomes often being averted by the adults who noticed and cared enough to step in and make a difference."

Will Evans, Director of Safety Education
Markell Insurance Company
Glen Allen, Virginia

"This is a simple, elegant, and truly remarkable book that touched me deeply. It evoked deep anger, tears of sorrow and tears of triumph. This book should be required reading for every educator and parent in America. It is a powerful and timely message from one of our most respected experts on school safety. It is a brilliant analysis of bullying and school safety, and a clarion call for action."

Lieutenant Colonel Dave Grossman
Best selling author of *On Killing* and Coauthor of *Let's Stop Teaching Our Kids to Kill - a Call to Action Against TV, Movie & Video Game Violence*
Jonesboro, Arkansas

"*Weakfish* offers a glimpse of bullying that is nothing short of profound. Scores of state and federal government agencies, as well as officials from other countries, have turned to Michael Dorn for his expertise. Techniques he pioneered have been used to reduce crime, violence, weapons violations and even to avert planned school shootings and bombings in our schools. No other single individual has done more to shape and influence the face of school safety in the United States. His concepts are now in standard usage from Maine to California and as far away as Israel and Australia. Now, in this incredibly passionate and moving work, he offers a different type of crucial insight for those dedicated individuals who have accepted the challenge of educating, nurturing and safeguarding our children. Every person who works with children would be well advised to read this amazing book. Michael knows school safety and we should listen earnestly to his words of encouragement and advice. Our company has been pleased to support Michael in his crusade to make schools a safe haven for our children.

Charles Garrett, President
Garrett Metal Detectors
Garland, Texas

"The powerful presentation by you and your son Chris was overwhelmingly rated the best presentation of our 2002 annual conference. We look forward to having you present again at next year's conference. The bottom line is that bullying can happen anywhere to anyone at any time and Stephen's inspiring story will help everyone understand how easy it is to overlook. *Weakfish* will encourage everyone to examine personal experiences with an eye toward understanding and preventing not only the negative physical consequences but, perhaps more importantly, the mental anguish that accompanies bullying. Thank you for sharing this child's special story with us; thank you for becoming the compassionate, dedicated advocate that you are today and thanks especially for inspiring us all to become better human beings."

Michael J. Martin, Executive Director
National Association for Pupil Transportation
Albany, New York

"*Weakfish* chronicles the struggle faced by 1 in 10 students in schools today who are faced with bullying and harassment on a regular basis. The book paints a realistic picture of a young man as he works through the turbulent and murky waters of nonacceptance and his fight to survive and be counted. The author is eloquent in his approach in dealing with a very complex problem in schools today while at the same time demonstrating through his writing a powerful simplicity in purpose...recognition of the pain and suffering that occurs through unconstrained bullying, harassment and student-on-student aggression with the eventual triumph that combines the strength of the human spirit and the compassion of a concerned adult who demonstrated that one person can make a difference. This book reconfirms that, regardless of the circumstances, good things happen to good people. As an administrator and practitioner who has worked in the field of crisis intervention and school violence for over twenty years, I was truly moved by the author's sincerity. A must read for any school-based practitioner, school resource officer, teacher, school administrator or parent. Just like his powerful and motivating live presentation on the same topic, *Weakfish* delivers 150%"

Bill Miller
Crisis/Threat Assessment Team Administrator,
School Psychologist
Clark County School District
Las Vegas Nevada

"This short but powerful book at first evokes a fable-like quality but soon relates experiences so horrifying that they must be real. The story culminates in a revelation that will astonish readers and inspire them to redouble their efforts to strengthen the nets that protect our weakfish from the barracudas that would devour them. Every parent and every adult who works with young people in our schools should view the problem of bullying from the unique perspective of *Weakfish*."

Mary C. Noshang, Editor in Chief
Today's School and *Today's Catholic School Teacher*
Dayton, Ohio

"*Weakfish* analyzes a complex and pervasive societal problem through compelling storytelling and powerful insights. A must read for the youth work professional."

R. Leslie Nichols, AIA,
Vice President
Boys and Girls Clubs of America
Member of the National Child Protection Task Force
Atlanta, Georgia

"This true story of Stephen will grip you with the emotions of sadness, embarrassment, anger and triumph. The reader will value all children as our 'greatest resource' and realize schools can be dangerous places for our kids."

Ted Poe, Judge 228th District Court
Well-known national speaker,
victim's rights advocate and humanitarian
Houston, Texas

"*Weakfish* is a powerful tale of how bullies ultimately don't win. It provides practitioners with practical insights and guidance on preventing and handling bullying in school."

Caroline Ryan, Editor
Maintaining Safe Schools
LRP Publications

"*Weakfish* leads us through the hills of bullying and the peaks that mount into tiers of pain. Through the eyes of a child, Michael Dorn commands us toward the summit of solutions by offering a unique perspective and ubiquitous insights into a vast land that we see every day yet some choose to ignore. *Weakfish* speaks volumes to address the manner in which unworldly ignorance can be so profound that it can destroy the fibers of innocence. This book proclaims hope and endurance as swords and shields in our battle to reclaim our youth. My colleague Michael Dorn is truly the master of the school safety arena and a passionate advocate for our kids."

Sonayia N. Shepherd MS
Chief Operating Officer
Safe Havens International Inc.
Atlanta, Georgia

Other Books Authored and Co-authored by Michael Dorn

Innocent Targets - When Terrorism Comes to School
By Michael and Chris Dorn
Safe Havens International Inc.

Let None Learn in Fear
Spring 2006. Safe Havens International Inc.

The Last Straw – A Guide to Hate Groups, Cults, Youth Gangs
and Warning Signs of Destructive Youth Behaviors
By Michael Dorn, Chris Dorn and Sonayia Shepherd
Spring 2006. Safe Havens International Inc.

Sexual Monsters – What Every Parent, Educators and Youth
Service Professional Must Know About Child Molesters
By Michael Dorn, Chris Dorn and Russell Bentley
Fall, 2006. Safe Havens International Inc.

Jane's Safe Schools Planning Guide for All Hazards
Jane's Teacher Safety Guide
Jane's School Safety Handbook: Second Edition
www.janes.com or 1-800-824-0768

School/Law Enforcement Partnerships:
A Guide to Police Work in Schools
Ram Publishing. Available from Save Havens International Inc.

Policing and Crime Prevention
Deborah Mitchell Robinson, Editor
Prentice Hall *www.prenhall.com/policestore*

School Safety Essentials - Series of twelve short books
LRP Publishing. 1-800-341-7874 extension 275

Warriors – On Livings with Courage, Discipline, and Honor
Edited by Loren W. Christenson. Paladin Press. *www.paladin-press.com*

"The right way to begin is to pay attention to the young, and make them just as good as possible."

—Socrates

Preface

For continuity, the author's observations are in lighter type text and the narrative of Stephen's story is printed in bold type. As will be explained more fully in the story, the terms "weakfish" and "barracuda" are used as metaphors to evoke a parallel situation involving the dangers bullied children face and the need to develop a safe environment for our youth. The use of male gender pronouns for bullies, i.e. "barracudas", and victims, i.e. "weakfish" is in no way meant to imply that only the male gender demonstrates those behaviors and characteristics. Indeed, experience and research have shown otherwise.

The original draft of the manuscript included specific names of schools involved. Reviewers felt that naming of the individual schools described could tend to serve as an indictment of those dedicated educators who happened to be assigned to work in these particular schools. I would hasten to point out that the situations described in this book are still common in some schools today in spite of improvements in school safety. While educators and school employees now receive considerably more preparation to recognize different learning styles and destructive youth behavior, many are still not given adequate preparation or support to address the many safety-related challenges they face in the classroom.

Stephen

Stephen was in most regards a regular boy growing up in an ordinary house in a typical neighborhood. He was a bright child who liked to play. He enjoyed interaction with other children and found school to be a particularly fun and interesting place. The little boy liked to read and ponder, and, probably more than anything else, he loved to play in the woods near his home, to wander and explore them. Climbing trees, jumping through puddles and sitting in grass thickets watching for wildlife were his favorite pastimes. It was during these adventures that he fantasized about being a pioneer, an archaeologist or, sometimes, even a courageous explorer.

On one balmy spring day when Stephen was in the second grade, he was enjoying a romp in the woods near his home in Buffalo, New York, just as he always did. As he conquered new territory in the Wild West and his trusty horse rode up just in the nick of time to help him save the day, something terrible happened to Stephen that would forever alter his life. For on this day, Stephen was set upon by two youths. The boys were not in the woods to play, nor were they enjoying the wildlife. These teens were predators, the kind of young people who know right from wrong, but don't care. Surely, these young men had influences in their lives that steered them on a path of destruction. They would be described as "at risk" by social scientists, but, to Stephen, they were vicious. Compared to Stephen, they were giants, appearing 10-feet tall, but their size mattered not because their terrible intentions exceeded their stature when they found the little boy alone in the woods. Sexual molestation was the name of their game, and Stephen was the player, victim and, in this game, the loser. The terrible things that these boys did to Stephen would change the manner in which he viewed himself, other children and the world around him. Indeed, the woods that the little boy had frequented became forevermore a frightful place on that sunny day. For Stephen, the good times that he had cherished in those woods ceased to exist as abruptly as a thunderclap with the horror of what the young predators did to him. While they were likely victims of sexual abuse themselves, we each have the power to choose to continue the cycle or to end it.

Stephen

Like many victims of sexual molestation and sexual assault, Stephen did not report this tragic event. He did not tell his parents or his siblings. He did not call the police because, like many such victims, he did not fully comprehend what had happened to him nor what should be done about it. After all, he was only a small child. Because he did not tell of these events, he did not receive assistance from those who have helped heal such emotional wounds. No counselor or psychologist was able to help the boy, for he did not seek their assistance. He was, after all, just an ordinary little boy faced with a situation that he did not create nor comprehend, but only knew was "bad."

As with many children and adults who fall prey to sexual predators, Stephen tried to go it alone, to cope and to carry on with his life. He did not tell a sibling nor did he speak of the happening to his parents. Being but a child, he did not know to summon the police, and, because they were not called, he did not receive the help from those healers in our society – the mental health professionals who can help a child cope with such devastating occurrences. He simply went about the business of being a little boy as best he knew how. Of course, you and I know that Stephen, like any other child in such a situation, was profoundly affected. In fact, the events of that sunny spring day would not only have an effect on Stephen, but on others as well.

Stephen returned to his school the next day. He viewed that place, too, in a different light now. He still enjoyed school, but something had changed.

We know that a school is but a microcosm of a community. School reflects the best and the worst of what is in our society. Excellent teachers bring out the very best in our children while they are in school. Our doctors, scientists, nurses, police officers, soldiers, mayors, governors and even our presidents develop in this environment.

Research tells us that school-aged children are among the most at -risk groups in our society for many things. They are more likely than most of us to commit, as well as to be victimized in, crimes such as sexual assault, robbery, physical assault and murder. When we take this high-risk group and put them into the building we call a school, we must be mindful that the risk is still there. In fact, some research indicates that many children report that they are more frequently victims of crime at school than in any other setting.

While Stephen was, of course, unfamiliar with any such research, he did now feel something at school that he had never experienced, fear of his classmates. For Stephen was now aware that other children could indeed harm him.

A Change of Scenery

That summer, Stephen's father accepted a job in a faraway place. His new job would pay him a higher salary and would allow him to provide a better life for his family. So it was that Stephen found himself settling into a new home, a new neighborhood and a new life. The next fall, Stephen began school in a different town called Dothan, Alabama. Stephen would describe his new school as a nice looking building in a well-kept neighborhood. Stephen would tell us that his was a school where the average student, parent or teacher would probably not have much concern over safety when they saw this place. The school was in good condition and was kept spotlessly clean. The surrounding neighborhood gave way to a picturesque image of a typical American neighborhood, the American middle-class dream. The serene houses stood tall to Stephen, and lawns were manicured and hedges trimmed. This was indeed a postcard picture of Americana.

Keep in mind that schools like Heritage High School in Conyers, Georgia; Pearl High School in Pearl, Mississippi; and Columbine High School in Jefferson County, Colorado, are all very nice schools in nice neighborhoods. In fact, they are all good schools attended by bright students, taught by good teachers and led by capable administrators. They are also schools where there was perhaps little perceived risk and there were not adequate measures in place to safeguard the children in them. Apparently, no one realized the hazards, or, if they did, they did not act upon their concerns. Horrible acts of violence took place in each of these schools. Some of the most dangerous schools in our great nation are housed in the nicest buildings in the best parts of town. They are dangerous not because the inherent threat level is high but, instead, because appropriate safety measures are not perceived to be necessary.

Stephen would find that, although his nice new school had fresh paint and shiny floors, it was a dark and hostile place. For, as soon as he began to attend the third grade, he found himself singled out because of his prominent northern accent. The little boy did not understand why some of his classmates acted as they did toward him. He could not comprehend what he should do about the increasing intensity of their aggression each day. He saw other instances of children being taunted and teased, but it seemed as if his experiences were somehow different, more frequent and more persistent in nature. He wondered why these youth had such a dislike for people from the North. He struggled with a means to understand and for the best way to cope with the situation.

Bullies pick on others for a variety of reasons. Children (and adults) are targeted because they act differently, talk differently, have physical disabilities or are of a different race, religion or culture. Bullies pick on those who dress differently, listen to different music or seem to have different sexual preferences. Bullies often target those who are different in almost any way, real or imagined. A Georgia middle school student died after being punched and kicked as he departed from his school bus. The child responsible for his death had, in many prior instances, attacked smaller boys. The bully repeatedly accused his victims of being gay, even when there was no indication that they were. A high percentage of bullying relates to real or perceived differences in sexual orientation. In any instance, the bullying behavior is harmful and should not be tolerated. In the same school district, another child committed suicide with a handgun at school after he was also tormented by bullies.

Of course, Stephen did not know this about the selection methods or prevalence of bullies. He only knew that he was continually teased and taunted because of how he talked.

Like many children, Stephen probably reacted to these acts of aggression in a manner that brought even more bullying upon him. Such children frequently become the targets of increased bullying as they draw more and more attention upon themselves because of the way they react. While we should engage in efforts to teach our children how to respond appropriately to such aggression, I propose that the burden should not be on the child to respond to bullying; instead the responsibility should lie squarely on the shoulders of the "big people" in the school to create an environment that is not conducive to such activities. This type of environment has been and can be created by caring adults who will accept no less for children.

> In Stephen's case, the bullying intensified with each school day. The hostility grew, culminating in an attack when two of Stephen's classmates assaulted him on the playground during recess. The boys who punched Stephen as they called him "Yankee" were mere children, third graders, but we must understand just how painful an experience it can be for a small child to be attacked in such a manner.

When a ten-year-old child was bullied in such a fashion in a Montana elementary school, he was forced by the "big people" to shake hands with his tormentors. On the next day, he returned to school with a handgun and opened fire. He missed the child at whom he was shooting and killed instead an 11-year-old bystander. While we can never condone or accept a child's carrying a weapon to school because he or she is bullied or threatened, we must understand cause and effect in such situations. While there were obviously other factors in this child's life to evoke such a reaction, we cannot afford to miss the correlation between the environment and the resulting violence. If we allow bullying and low-level violence in our schools, we should not be surprised when a shooting, stabbing or other weapons assault takes place. We must make certain choices about safety in our schools. Children die most often when we allow conditions to exist that are precursors to this type of violence. We must be advocates for all of our children, not just those whom we like or enjoy having in our schools and in our communities.

A high school student named Randy was one such youth. Randy was repeatedly teased and bullied in his Georgia high school, but there was no advocate for Randy. He planned for several days what he would do. Randy made a poor choice. He rode the bus to school one day with more than 90 pounds of guns, knives and an explosive device that he had constructed. Randy fired shots and took other students hostage. Fortunately, Randy was subdued by several of his hostages after a lengthy standoff with sheriff's deputies, and no one was killed. Cause and effect were in operation here. A series of tragedies turned into a bigger loss for Randy and for his community. Other tragic situations have occurred around the country and in other nations. A New Hampshire student who was bullied by an athlete entered the school with a full-length shotgun partially concealed under his coat, took hostages and was shot and killed in a gunfight with responding police officers, two of whom were permanently disabled during the shootout. A close call occurred in the early 1990s in a small West Virginia middle school when a student who had been bullied approached a group of football players with several handguns concealed in his waistband intent on opening fire. Fortunately, he was subdued before he could begin his shooting rampage. The situation is also of concern for institutions of higher learning where a number of shooting sprees have occurred with as many as 14 victims killed in one shooting rampage in Canada. In one incident at a state university, a student who was criminally bullied shot his tormentor and committed suicide after university police handled his complaint "administratively," referring it to the Dean of Students rather than to a court of law. The victim felt, and the perpetrator demonstrated by his actions, that it was not likely that action by the Dean's office would have any impact on the situation. The common practice of the university to try to avoid using arrest as a means to handle criminal acts by students was intended to reduce instances where students had criminal records hindering employment opportunities after graduation. The end result, of course, was the tragic loss of the lives of two young men. The implications for our society from these situations are immense.

> When Stephen was punched on the playground, his already tainted view of school would change even more. The child who had loved school so much would now begin to see school as a place where other children could and would physically harm him. Again, a case of cause and effect.
>
> Stephen's problems with academics had been increasing over time, so his parents heeded the advice of his teachers and had the boy tested for learning disabilities. The tests revealed that Stephen had dyslexia and was hyperactive (what we commonly refer to as ADHD). Research shows that children with these types of disabilities are more likely to face chronic bullying. Stephen, like many children, did not have the type of relationship with his parents that made him inclined to

speak with them about what was really at the root
of most of his problems in school.

Respite

As Stephen began to dislike his new school and fear other children, something happened: he changed schools. Stephen learned that he would be attending a different school, farther from his home. The school district was redrawing district lines, and Stephen was rezoned to attend a different school. Upon approaching his new school for the first time, he found that it was in a different kind of neighborhood. This school was in a neighborhood that could only be described as one that might cause us to be concerned if we drove through it at night. The neighborhood was run-down. The neighborhood was a scary place to a little boy. When he arrived at the school, Stephen found it to be in disrepair. Stephen would depict this school to us as one that, at first glance, might make a student, parent or teacher apprehensive. When Stephen entered the school on that first day, he quickly realized that there was something else quite different about this school: he was one of but five white children in the school. Now you should understand that Stephen's father was perhaps not the most culturally sensitive of men, for he sometimes used racial slurs and made derogatory comments in front of his son when he spoke of people of other cultures, races and religions. Stephen's childhood ensured that he readily noticed that his color did not match everyone else's. All fathers have faults, just as they have attributes, for they are, like each of us, human. Of course, we all know well that a small boy can be heavily influenced by his father, in both positive and negative ways. Because of this, Stephen was now even more apprehensive about his new school. After all, here was a child who had been tormented, even attacked, because he spoke differently from other children. In this new school, he was also of a different color from most of his peers, and his perceived notions added a sense of panic to his situation. Naturally, Stephen was afraid; he expected trouble. Oddly enough though, Stephen would notice as each day passed that none of his fears materialized. These children were not as his father had described them, nor were they like the children in his last school. Day by day, Stephen began to relax and to enjoy school again, and he even started to interact once more with other children. The little boy no longer felt afraid.

Although he looked starkly different from most of his classmates, he did not feel different, nor was he treated differently. For Stephen, that made all of the difference in the world.

As time passed, Stephen, being an intelligent and reflective child, began to ponder on his new sense of safety. He began to consider what exactly made him feel safer and more at ease in this run-down school in a worn neighborhood. Finally, it struck Stephen that the principal was the cause of his new lease on life. The principal, it seemed, was subject to appear at any moment at any place in the school. The principal would pop up in class-rooms, in the library (Stephen's favorite place in the school), in the cafeteria or on the playground. Stephen also realized that there always seemed to be an adult within earshot or eyesight. At any given moment, a teacher, custodian, librarian or other "big person" was close at hand. He also noticed that the adults in the school seemed to be keenly aware of the children, much more so than at any school that he had attended. Whenever a student acted in an untoward fashion, made an inappropriate comment about another child or acted in some other inappropriate manner, an adult would quickly intervene and correct the situation. The school climate was warm and caring. Stephen felt safe there. So it was that the little boy began to enjoy school again, to learn and to play as children are supposed to in their schools.

Small People, Big Difference

Then, one day after school, Stephen found himself confronted by an older youth, a much larger boy from Stephen's own neighborhood. Stephen found that on this occasion there was no adult on the school grounds to intervene on his behalf. The bully pushed and shoved Stephen, shattering his newfound sense of safety like a delicate champagne glass when dropped on the floor. However, just as the bully was about to move in for the attack, something happened that Stephen would never forget. Several older youths, children Stephen did not know, children from a different neighborhood, intervened on his behalf. These young men placed themselves between Stephen and the aggressor and told the bully in clear terms that he had best leave the little boy alone. The bully backed down and never bothered Stephen again.

I have worked with many schools around the country and in other nations to improve the level of safety for our children and those who dedicate their lives to educating them. I have seen numerous successful examples of schools where students are allowed and encouraged to help enhance the level of safety. In the district where I had the privilege of serving as chief of school police, Superintendent Thomas Hagler took the then bold step of asking students to participate on a school safety task force. We were struggling with the issue of weapons on our campus in the early 1990s. My officers were confiscating more than 400 weapons a year from our 25,000 students. Most of these weapons were recovered due to tips from other students. We were beginning to learn that while student tips are an important means to recover weapons brought to school by students, it is, in fact, the least efficient means to do so. Our school district was experiencing stabbing incidents each year and believed that it was just a matter of time before a shooting occurred. As we forged ahead to find more effective methods to reduce the presence of weapons in our schools, we began to research entry-point metal detection as an option. Entry-point metal detection is the method commonly utilized at airports, courthouses and other facilities. We had serious misgivings as to the effectiveness of this concept for our situation.

While all of us "professional types" were discussing the results of our research into metal detection at a community school safety task force meeting, a student asked a seemingly naive question. He asked, "Why do you have to check every student each morning?" He went on to ask, "Why couldn't you draw classroom numbers and check each student in the selected classrooms with a metal detector? That way, students would never know when they would be checked." He pointed out that this method would deter most students from carrying a weapon without requiring students to come to school early each day to stand in line to be checked. Upon further research, we found that the student's question was, in fact, a brilliant idea, and a random metal detection program was implemented. Now, more than a decade later, student weapons violations have dropped by more than 90 percent, and the program has strong support from students, parents and staff. Many districts across the country now use the same method with similar results. As an aside, this concept has saved the district more than $50 million when compared to the costs of entry-point metal detection over the years. Not bad work for a kid with a seemingly impractical question.

I have seen many other examples of valuable student contributions, student crime watch programs, peer-mediation programs, teen courts and other such student-centered approaches. In one case, a student attending a private school developed a CD-ROM pre-incident planning system (PIPS) to better prepare his school for emergencies. PIPS programs contain schematic drawings, photographs and even video tours of schools to enable public safety responders and school officials to respond more effectively to crisis situations such as a tornado strike, fire or hostage situation. Private vendors often charge several thousand dollars per school for such a program. This young man rose to the challenge to make his school a safer place.

> Stephen saw firsthand and on a very personal level what it means for a principal, his staff and students to create an environment where students decide to make their school a safer place. This

welcoming environment surrounded the boy like a warm blanket on a cold winter night. This little boy would always remember it.

Back Into the Fire

As fate would have it, just as Stephen was beginning to find school to once again be a pleasant and safe place, his father was laid off from his new job when his company lost a major contract. Being a dedicated provider for his family, he quickly found a new and better-paying position in another state, a chance once again to improve the standard of living for his family. Stephen's father always worked hard and long hours for his family; it was his way of expressing love for them. Once again, the little boy began to settle into a nice new house and a new neighborhood.

Stephen liked his new house, which was larger and had a bigger yard. His father had indeed provided better for his family. Stephen also liked his new neighborhood. He felt safe there, and there were woods nearby where he once again began to play on long summer days that seemed not to end.

The summer came and went, and, in the fall, the little boy enrolled in a new school in Macon, Georgia. Macon has been the home of many famous musicians, including singer Otis Redding and the Allman Brothers Band. Macon is also a community known for its beautiful pre-Civil War homes. Sadly, though, Stephen would once again find his new school to be a place where a child with a Northern accent was not welcomed by some.

Just as a child from Charleston, South Carolina, might be taunted in a New Jersey school because of a Southern accent, Stephen was again bullied because of his speech. To Stephen, it seemed at times as if the Civil War had just ended, and he was to blame for the differences between North and South.

Each day, the taunting grew more severe, and Stephen probably did not handle the situation as well as some other children might have.

We must not forget the impact that the little boy's experiences on that sunny day when he was molested may have had on his ability to interact with aggressive peers. Those who care for children should always be mindful that many youths have had experiences that prime them to respond unwisely. Caregivers should receive training to help them recognize at-risk youth like Stephen so early intervention can take place.

So it was that day by day, Stephen found himself at odds with more and more of the other children in his school.

The heckling and teasing escalated until the fourth grader was again physically attacked by his peers, by children who should have been his new friends. Stephen was attacked not just once, but on numerous occasions. He was attacked on the school grounds in the afternoons, and, in several instances, he was beaten up in the neighborhood as he tried to make his way home. One afternoon, Stephen was even attacked on his very own doorstep. The little boy would now find his fear of school expand to his travels to and from school.

This is a common predicament for many children, one that can have a profound effect on the real and perceived level of safety in a school. Even children who feel safe while in the classroom may bring a gun to school for fear of what may happen as they make their way to and from the campus. Crime around a school erodes the feeling of safety our children need in order to focus on learning and growing. We all know that when a child is shot to death across the street from a school, students and teachers feel no safer than if the tragedy had taken place in a classroom or in the gymnasium.

So it was that with each passing day, Stephen would find uncertainty in his travels to and from this place that became more and more unpleasant for him. Day by day his fear and dislike for his school would fester like a wound that did not heal in his soul.

The Barracuda

By the time Stephen entered the sixth grade, things had not improved. In fact, things had become much worse. For a new child—a barracuda—entered his school.

Now, when I speak of children as "barracudas" and "weakfish," I mean no disrespect to Stephen or to either type of child for that matter. I use the analogy to help others understand certain dynamics that sometimes take place between two types of children. Having much experience with children who fall prey to their peers and with those who prey upon them, I use this comparison to help people understand an aspect of bullying that is different from what they may hear elsewhere.

If we go to the ocean and observe a large school of small fish, they may appear to us to be simply a large school of small fish. The fish appear to us as wonders of nature and the world around us as they make their way through the sea. In the same ocean, we may also see certain predatory fish, like the barracuda. However, the barracuda does not see as we do a large school of small fish. Instead, to the barracuda, certain specific fish within the school immediately stand out. While we would observe the school of fish as a whole, the barracuda sees only the weakfish. The barracuda has the ability to quickly spot those fish that appear to be weaker, and the barracuda will attack these weakfish because they are easy prey. They appear weaker because they swim a little differently, act uniquely in some other subtle fashion or exhibit some other difference that sets them apart from the other fish.

So it is with children. Most of us see simply beautiful little children, the wonders of our species, but, in our society and in schools, there are predators who quickly spot the vulnerable children in the crowd. A child molester prowling a shopping mall can often quickly single out that one child who is vulnerable. In our schools, predatory children can also spot with ease the "different" one who may be their next victim.

Now, if we were to take a school of fish from the great blue sea and put it into a custom-built aquarium, much as we take children from a neighborhood and place them in a big building we call a school, the fish would remain together much as children do. If we were also to take a three-foot barracuda and place it in the aquarium, it would seek out and attack the weakfish. In the same fashion, when we place hundreds of children from that high-risk age group in our society into a school, some will prey upon others if we allow it.

We can change the environment in our aquarium. We can build a net for our aquarium. Now, we must custom build this net because our aquarium, you see, is different from any other. We cannot go to a pet shop or department store and simply buy a net. No store will have a net of the precise dimensions for our unique aquarium. The net must fit the dimensions of the aquarium exactly, lest the barracuda slip between the net and the sides. We must construct the net of materials that are sturdy enough to resist the strength of this powerful fish, or it may break through to attack the weakfish. We must also make the holes in the net of such dimensions that the barracuda cannot pass through it.

If we build the net with great care, the little fish will be safe from the sharp teeth of the barracuda. Certainly, a little fish may from time to time venture through the net and be at risk. For the most part though, our little fish will be free from the dangers of the barracuda.

So it is with a school. If we take great care and love and pay close attention to detail, we can craft a safety net for our children in each school and, in fact, in the neighborhood that surrounds it. I have seen this done with great success. We must understand that it is not an easy task to build a safety net for our children. It takes great commitment to make such a net. While we as a society care deeply for our children and those who work with children care greatly for them, today's world requires a great deal of us if we want our youth to be safe. Only when advocates for our children are willing to toil long and hard will such a net be prepared.

Just as our net in the aquarium, a safety net for children cannot simply be purchased. There is no product, nor services that will eliminate the necessity of our hard work. Our schools are unique—even when two schools in the same community are constructed using identical building plans. Every school has its own strengths and weaknesses. There are many products and experts available to help us ease the way, to guide us and to serve as valuable materials for the construction of our net. Nevertheless, in the end, we must actively participate in building the net through our own efforts.

Now, we can attempt to build this safety net ourselves, as is often done, from a single perspective, one person's viewpoint. Some schools rely on metal detectors, others on surveillance cameras. Many of our schools place great value on school resource officers, and yet many more rely upon programs designed to modify the behavior of students in more gentle ways. Those entrusted with our youth have implemented a wide range of approaches so that no harm comes to the children they serve. While each of these measures has a time and place in which it can provide significant benefit, none alone will suffice. There have been major acts of violence in schools that have metal detectors or school resource officers and/or bullying prevention programs as well, and we have seen very clearly recorded images of students on shooting rampages from schools with elaborate security camera systems. In fact, we have seen major safety failures in many schools with a limited focus in their approach to safety.

There is another option for the manner in which a safety net is constructed. For many years, Dr. Ronald Stephens, the Executive Director of the National School Safety Center, has recommended a community-based multidisciplinary approach to the development of a comprehensive school safety strategy. We can bring together the perspectives of those from different disciplines and and build our net together. A school administrator, a police officer, a school mental health worker and a parent can each have a significant and positive impact on the level of safety in a school. These same people working together as a team will have far greater power to effect positive change than all of their actions if taken separately.

Of course, when we work together to build a safety net, we must be mindful that it has to be carefully maintained with great love and care. Safety for our children is not a one-time affair. We cannot simply design and craft our safety net as a one-shot solution to our concerns. Indeed, the net in an aquarium will rot if not maintained, exposing our little fish to danger as time lapses. So it is with safety nets for our schools. The nets will demand constant vigilance and attention, or they too will rot.

In fact, safety nets will need to be continually mended to withstand new dangers. In an aquarium, the barracuda may give birth to hundreds of new predatory fish. These small barracuda will slip through the net and victimize little fish unless we modify the net to meet the new threat.

The safety net for our children is no different. From time to time, new threats will emerge that threaten the peacefulness of our schools. Currently, we are aware that our schools are more vulnerable to acts of terrorism. While we have had two incidents of domestic terrorism in American elementary schools in years past, we must be aware that the dangers of international terrorism in our schools have increased. We know that terrorists in other countries have repeatedly selected schools as targets for their bloody acts. In a November 1999 press conference, a ranking U.S. military officer announced that documents were seized in terrorist training camps in Afghanistan that described schools as potential targets of trainees. While the chances of any particular school being selected as a target by terrorists are remote, we must be mindful that a single horrific incident of terrorism in an elementary school in a town that most of us have never heard of would cause immediate terror for students, educators and parents across our great land. So we must further mend our safety net to address this enhanced threat.

Whatever the new particular threat in a given time period, we have to be prepared to make adjustments on a regular basis. While security cameras or metal detectors may not be deemed to be appropriate in a given school this year, they may be needed next year as the threat level changes. Communities that are not prepared to adjust to new threats will allow additional fear to permeate and impede the learning process.

There will always be children in our schools who seem at first glance by an untrained eye to be just like the other, "ordinary" children. Just as the weakfish in the school of fish stands out instantly to the barracuda, these children stand out readily to predatory children. In a school of fish, the barracuda may pick out subtle differences, such as a slightly different swimming motion, or there may be more overt signs. A fish that has been injured may swim on its side on the surface unable to right itself. The barracuda will instantly home in on such a fish. Those who fish for recreation understand this concept well, as many fishing lures are designed to imitate injured fish. There are children who give off such overt cues as well. These children will be set upon just as rapidly as the injured minnow in the sea if the school's safety net is not up to par. Unless those who work with children are properly trained and alert to recognize the signs of the weakfish, they will fall prey to the barracuda as well. Our nation's teachers, youth ministers, doctors, nurses, police officers, Little League coaches, scout leaders and countless others who interact with children must learn what to look for and remain ever vigilant for those children in need of intervention and support, whether they be weakfish or barracuda. Of course our parents, aunts, uncles, grandparents, brothers, sisters and especially our youth themselves must be ready to do their part for their relatives, friends and loved ones.

The movement to address bullying in this country and abroad is gaining momentum. Though much work remains to be done, more and more are joining in the honorable, crucial quest to end bullying in our communities and schools. From the Silence Hurts™ Campaign that began in Florida to the recently announced American Medical Association stance on bullying as a health issue, more and more students, parents and professionals who work with youth are stepping up to the plate.

> Unfortunately, the movement had not yet begun during Stephen's youth in Macon, Georgia, when Stephen met the barracuda for the first time in his school. The barracuda in this case took the form of a tall slender youth with red hair. From the moment they met, Stephen could tell that this bully was different. He had a clear desire, willingness and ability to inflict pain far beyond that of those who had tormented Stephen in the past. He quickly singled out Stephen as a weakfish to be preyed upon.
>
> For Stephen, his elementary school quickly turned into a prison of fear. The barracuda would seize every opportunity to verbally and physically assault the smaller boy. No doubt there were other victims of his unwanted aggressions, but Stephen was obviously a favorite target.
>
> The barracuda was a natural master of the opportunities presented by negligent privacy.

Negligent privacy occurs when those who supervise and monitor children do not remain vigilant and unwittingly provide the opportunity for victimization to occur. Negligent privacy can occur on a playground filled with second graders, in a crowded high school cafeteria, during a youth group camping trip or even 10 feet away from a teacher in a classroom. Simply put, negligent privacy occurs when adults are not paying close attention to children under their care.

> In Stephen's case, the school bathroom was the place he feared most. Because Stephen had never seen an adult in the boys' bathroom, he felt more vulnerable there. The barracuda also apparently noted that school staff rarely ventured into the boys' bathroom and, like other predators young and old, became emboldened by his assurance that he would not be interfered with while harassing other students in the bathroom.

Both surveys of students and school incident reports highlight bathrooms as common problem areas. From bullying to bomb placement, bathrooms are high on the list of trouble spots in schools. Using the research-based concepts of crime prevention through environmental design (CPTED), properly trained architects can design bathrooms and other areas in a manner to reduce the real and perceived probability of crime. You have most likely seen CPTED rest rooms in buildings and not realized it. For example, many rest rooms of this type have no doors at the entryway. In a bathroom with a design that relies on the zigzag entrance layout to block the view from the hallway instead of one or more doors, an aggressor cannot depend on the sound of a door opening to warn him that someone else is approaching. At the same time, a potential victim knows that a call for help will be heard by people in the vicinity. Unfortunately, participant feedback during training sessions for a number of architects has revealed that many architects are still not familiar with the powerful concepts of CPTED. Still, no design features will totally eliminate the need for those who work with children to physically supervise them. Similarly, experience has shown that school staff may be more willing to frequently spot check student rest rooms when they are kept clean and odor free. CPTED emphasizes our use as well as the design of facilities.

Unfortunately for Stephen, there was no supervision of this poorly designed bathroom. The barracuda had little fear of any adult entering his torture chamber, and, even if the unexpected happened, there was always the squeaky door to sound the alarm. So the barracuda felt at ease while the weakfish's fear was magnified in this most dangerous of places in the school. Stephen would try to avoid going to the bathroom. Oh, how hard he would try! Of course, in spite of his best efforts, he would find that he would still sometimes have to use the rest room. On some of these occasions, the barracuda would catch him there.

Stephen underwent many trials and tribulations at the hands of the barracuda in that place, in that room filled with dark secrets. One day, the barracuda grew tired of simply pushing and striking Stephen. On that day, he ordered his frail victim to kneel on the bathroom floor. Stephen, by now utterly terrified

of the red-headed boy, complied. Next, the barracuda did something terrible. The barracuda ordered
Stephen to pretend to perform an act of oral sex on
the bully. In an act of sheer capitulation driven by
immense fear, the little boy complied. Now, the barracuda did not actually sexually molest Stephen, but
it is obvious that any child would be deeply affected
by this simulation paralleling his earlier humiliating
and painful experience. He would eventually lose
most of his remaining sense of self-worth, self-con-
fidence, dignity and pride. The barracuda seemed
to sense his further enhanced power and control
over the weakfish. The barracuda forced the little
boy to endure this humiliating ritual on a number of
occasions when he caught his hapless victim in the
bathroom. Other students sometimes witnessed
these events, adding to the degradation, but apparently no one reported these incidents to school
staff. Stephen certainly did not; he was gripped
by real and imaginary fears of what the barracuda
would do to him if he told anyone.

Many mental health and law enforcement professionals who work
with victims of sexual child molestation and exploitation would
note that the behavior of the barracuda indicates the likelihood that
this child also was a victim of sexual abuse. In fact, it is possible
that much of his behavior stemmed from such things. We must
take care in addressing those situations as well, for far too often,
we allow a barracuda to prey on others in our society because

we mistake sympathy with assistance. In many cases, we fail to hold previous victims of various types of abuse accountable for their own misdeeds when they opt to prey on others themselves. Often, we not only allow these individuals to multiply their own suffering by allowing them to victimize others, but we fail to force them to address their own issues through the support of consequences for their own actions.

Regardless of the barracuda's motivations, he was destroying Stephen's self-esteem with every encounter in the bathroom. As each day passed, Stephen grew to like school less and less. His academic performance revealed Stephen's distress. His performance at school declined, just as his parents and teachers had feared due to the test results showing that he had learning disabilities.

Near the end of the school year, another instance of negligent privacy took place. While Stephen was in a class one day, his teacher told the class that she would be leaving the room for "just a minute or two." On occasion, people who are responsible to children forget that a great deal can happen in a short period of time when children are not being properly supervised. Of course, the teacher used the time-honored tradition of leaving a trustworthy student in charge of the class during her brief absence.

On this occasion, unfortunately, another child was also in the class—the barracuda. Though not through an intentional act, the teacher in effect left a child predator in charge of her classroom on that day, and, as soon as she departed, the barracuda stood up and approached Stephen's desk. Stephen was mortified. He knew instinctively that something very bad was about to happen to him; what it would be he could only imagine. As soon as the barracuda approached his desk, he ordered Stephen to stand, and he, of course, complied in utter terror. His knees were shaking, his lips quivering and his eyes were watering as he waited for his pain. The barracuda then told Stephen to kneel on the floor in front of the entire class.

We give our children much advice when it comes to bullying. We all know of situations where children have been told to "stand up to the bully," and in some situations, in the right context and at the right time, this can be sage and appropriate advice. In other cases, children who have followed this advice have died for it—even in our schools.

When Stephen mustered all of his strength to stand up to the bully, he quickly learned that he would pay a price for his assertiveness. He would learn a powerful lesson demonstrating how bullies control their prey.

A bully in a school can be but a smaller version of a bully of nations. Adolf Hitler was one such bully. More than 11 million Jews and ethnic minorities would die so he could maintain control of his evil empire. Joseph Stalin would cause or allow the deaths of millions of his own people during his reign and was never reluctant to squelch any form of resistance, however slight. So it is with a bully in a classroom to a much smaller extent. The barracuda feels compelled to demonstrate his power over others through the use of violence.

As soon as Stephen stood up to the bully, he was immediately and violently attacked. During this blitzkrieg in the classroom, the bully rolled over the little boy like Hitler's armored divisions rolled over Poland, Belgium and France. During the attack, the barracuda smashed Stephen's head into the hard classroom floor causing a concussion and a bleeding head wound. With his victim prostrate on the floor, the barracuda admonished the horrified witnesses, "best not tell...or else" before taking his seat with his position as tyrant of the school reestablished.

True to her word, the teacher returned to the classroom moments later to find one little boy staggering to his feet, blood oozing from his head. Logically, she asked the class what had taken place. No one would reply. She then asked Stephen how he had been injured. The weakfish looked into the sinister eyes of the barracuda before making his reply. You did not have to be in the room that day to know what his reply was. The little boy used one of the most common of all replies by the physically abused. Whether the victim is a child who has been beaten up by gang members or a woman who has been battered by an abusive husband, school officials, police officers, inquisitive doctors and suspicious judges have all heard the untruthful response, "I fell down."

Stephen's teacher, principal, the emergency room doctor and his mother believed his fear-inspired falsehood—a lie that burned him to the core and tugged at his very soul. Having to lie to protect someone who had and would continue to harm him so much made an already unjust situation even more unbearable.

Under the criminal code of the State of Georgia, this assault is classified as an aggravated assault. Thus, the incident constituted a very serious felony-grade crime. This devastating attack was witnessed by numerous school children, none of whom apparently reported the incident after the class ended. In addition, a relentless search of the files of the Macon Police Department would find no police report on this serious crime that occurred that day at this typical elementary school. Likewise, a meticulous perusal of the records of the public school system would again reveal no mention of the crime. Just like a significant percentage of the millions of crimes committed on school property in this country each year, this violent attack remained unreported to school and law enforcement officials. We cannot address problems that have not been identified. Uncovering problems with our youth and in our schools requires extreme vigilance and a willingness to question suspicious circumstances as well as assumptions.

To Stephen, his near-death experience in the classroom that day would intensify his perception of school as a prison of fear. He would return to school a severely broken child who felt as if he were serving a 12-year sentence for a crime he did not commit.

Stephen did not understand what he had done to deserve this treatment, these deplorable conditions. He could not identify his transgression—only his terror. Stephen would return each day to his school fearing greatly for his life. Other children have not been so lucky. In rare cases, they have died in similar situations. Though Stephen did not physically die that day, he knew that he easily could have, and his spirit and dignity did die.

So often we hear references to concerns not to "turn schools into prisons" when there is discussion about the use of such things as metal detectors, security cameras, access control systems, dress codes and school resource officers to enhance the level of safety in our schools. Sometimes, this mantra is an excuse rather than a reason. School resource officers have successfully thwarted many attempted or planned school weapons assaults, and, according to an independent study by the staff of the Silence Hurts™ Campaign, more than 90 percent of Florida high school students surveyed selected the school resource officer as the most trusted adult on campus. Metal detectors have helped to reduce school weapons violations by as much as 90 percent, allowing students to focus on their studies rather than watching their backs. Most people do not feel like a prisoner when they conduct transactions at their local bank under the watchful eye of numerous strategically placed security cameras, and many of us use a card access control system to enter our place of work each day. However, for some reason, there are people who will readily accept security measures to protect us in almost any setting other than a school. Not every school needs these and other similar types of security measures. On the other hand, more than two decades of experience working with more than 2,000 schools across the country and reviewing information on more than 1,000 acts of campus violence have made it crystal clear to me that far more schools need and do not have these measures than have them and do not need them.

There are still regions of the country where we place unarmed police officers in our schools to protect our children and staff. In just one large school system, two people have been shot in the presence of unarmed school district police officers who were helpless to prevent the tragic assaults before the decision was made to arm the officers. There are other examples of the same situation from around the country. There is no safe way for an unarmed educator, security officer or school resource officer to search a student for weapons. No training or techniques can overcome the inherent danger of this type of situation. We have seen dozens of instances at schools around the country where this reckless approach has resulted in injury, death or a hostage situation. Yet there are still those who roll the dice with the lives of educators and students by insisting that this clearly unsafe practice be continued in the name of school image. The focus on political correctness as a bigger priority than the real level of safety has resulted in the deaths of a number of school children and educators that could have been prevented. Still, in many communities, concern for image rules the day, while children try to learn in fear.

So it would be for Stephen as he returned to his prison each day. He would try to focus on the day when he would be rid of this terrible fear, this fear that gripped him while at his elementary school.

Moving Up

At the end of his last year of elementary school, Stephen's parents announced that he would be attending a private school with a good reputation for academic excellence and for solid discipline. His parents had become concerned about Stephen's lack of progress in school. They were unimpressed with the quality of education and the apparent lack of discipline in area schools, so, like many parents in the community, they turned to a private school as an alternative. Several of Stephen's teachers remarked to him that he was very fortunate that he would not be attending the middle school for which he was zoned for the next school year. They told Stephen that the private school he would be attending was an excellent school and that he was indeed lucky.

Over the summer, Stephen began to hope that this new school would be the answer to his dilemma.

He eagerly anticipated the beginning of the school year for the first time in many seasons. Soon enough, the new school year began.

Stephen found his new school to be a very orderly place with a strict academic regimen. The school administration had taken great care to create a disciplined and orderly environment, and the complex class schedule system resulted in a daily rotation of the order in which classes were attended. This system made each day more interesting. Students were well-dressed, and the school was clean.

Unfortunately, Stephen quickly learned that there were bullies in this school as well. So, for the first time, Stephen began to carry a weapon to school each day for protection, but he was never caught with the switchblade knife at school.

He also experienced a new reason to dislike the school when he became aware that many of the children at the school were from affluent families and shunned students who were not from such backgrounds. Lacking the designer clothing worn by many of his peers, he realized that many of the students did not welcome him into their cliques.

A number of authorities on bullying point out that when students are ostracized in this fashion, danger can result. Cliques can form with band members, football players, cheerleaders, the well-to-do or a host of different groups within the school. A female student who shot a classmate in a private school in the Northeast cited this as her motivation. She stated that she shot her victim because the girl caused her to be shunned by peers. Again, while we cannot accept such provocations as justification for violence, we must understand and address the cause-and-effect relationship that they pose. Of course, such situations take place in both public and private schools.

One useful approach is to have faculty and staff members in a school attempt to identify those youth who do not seem to have a place in the school. Once this step has been taken, efforts are made to try to encourage these youth to become actively involved in at least one group in the school. This type of inclusion can make a tremendous difference for the individual child as well as for the environment of the school. A serious effort must be made to link every child in the school with a supportive peer group. Of course, consistent and comprehensive efforts must be undertaken to help all staff and students understand and buy into the idea of providing support for every student in the school.

Rebellion

Stephen never truly felt connected with his new classmates. He felt very much out of place in the school. As time passed, he decided that he no longer wished to attend this school. He wanted to be back in public schools where he did at least have a few friends from his neighborhood to whom he could relate. When he informed his parents of his desires, they told him that they had worked very hard to get him into this elite private school and that he would continue to attend it the following year. As with many middle school-aged youth, Stephen became rebellious and decided to force his parents to change their minds.

Stephen began to act out in school and virtually ceased any efforts to study. His teachers took note of his contempt for rules while his grades continued to fall. One of the nuns in the school often chastised him in front of his peers stating that he was "dead from his feet up and did not justify the air space he occupied." She also told the class that Stephen "would never amount to anything." Although she chided him in a friendly manner in an attempt to motivate him as she did with other underachieving students, he did not take her comments as motivational. Instead, she caused him to like the school even less.

By the end of the school year, Stephen had succeeded in clearly demonstrating that he did not wish to remain there and would not put forth any effort to pass his classes. His parents finally capitulated and told him that he could return to public school the following year. Stephen felt a sense of victory that would not last very long.

As the old saying goes, "Be careful what you wish for, because you just might get it." Stephen found that his new middle school was a far more dangerous school than any he had ever attended. The school was without a doubt an out of control school. Stephen quickly realized that there was little discipline in the school and that barracudas were much in evidence. He saw many violent fights and students using and selling drugs. Smoking and acts of vandalism were common.

Early in the school year, a group of students dismantled a boy's rest room on the ground floor of the school. Over a period of days, the boys removed the sinks, stall partitions and even the toilets from the bathroom. In spite of the severe water damage and removal of nearly every fixture in the rest room, apparently no one was caught, and no one was punished for these delinquent acts. Stephen on several occasions observed members of the same group emerge from the school carrying a bathroom fixture from the building to the area behind the school where students congregated during the lunch period. Their brashness conveyed a sense that students could do whatever they pleased at the school with little chance of facing consequences for their actions.

The following week, Stephen and other students watched in amazement as these same hoodlums tore down several hundred feet of fencing at the rear of the school property. They removed each piece and threw it down a hill behind the school. The students even ripped the metal fence posts from the ground and hurled them down the hillside. All of these acts happened in broad daylight, in front of many witnesses. Again, it appeared that none of the offenders were caught.

These events had a dramatic effect on the students in the school. Problems with discipline and violence increased as students apparently felt free to do as they pleased without consequence. Other students, particularly Stephen, became quite aware that they too could be the targets of the barracudas in the school. In short order, these fears materialized into fact.

Each day, students gathered outside of the building after lunch. The school was over the designed capacity by several hundred students, and they could not all remain in the cafeteria once they had finished eating. Instead, they would loiter outside of the building until the lunch period was over, if the weather permitted. One day, Stephen was approached by two students while he was waiting outside. One of the students produced a knife and threatened him with it. The students ordered Stephen to give them any money that he had, and they told him that they would stab him if he did not do so. Stephen had been in enough situations to know that they would carry out the threat if he did not comply, so he immediately relinquished his money. The students told him that they would kill him if he reported the incident and advised him to always give them all of his money when they requested it. They told him that they would cut him if they ever caught him withholding "their" money.

Again, Stephen knew better than to report the incident. From what he had seen at the school, it was clear that the principal was not in charge of the school: the barracudas reigned relentlessly and unchecked. The pair of thugs relieved Stephen of his money on numerous occasions. In fact, it quickly became quite clear that they only attended school to carry out their armed robberies. Stephen observed the two young men robbing other students on the grounds as well, making their rounds each day as though it was their regular job to do so. There are no police department reports on these armed robberies because Stephen did not report them. Dozens of armed robberies occurred at the middle school, in broad daylight, often witnessed by other students, yet these serious felony crimes appear in no statistical reports.

On one particular day, the pair of criminals approached Stephen and demanded "their" money. As was his usual practice, he immediately gave them every penny he had. These two barracudas were obviously experienced armed robbers, and they were skilled at their work. One of them threatened Stephen with his knife while his larger partner grabbed Stephen by his ankles and lifted the startled boy upside down with his head in the dirt. He shook Stephen while his knife wielding accomplice checked Stephen's pockets and underwear for hidden money. They removed his shoes and his socks seeking additional loot. Fortunately, Stephen had taken their threats seriously and was not holding back any funds, so they simply admonished him to be sure to continue to give up all that he had and dumped him on the ground before walking away to attend to other young and hapless victims.

Throughout the school year, Stephen would try to avoid danger only to find that it permeated the school. The lack of structure and discipline in the school bewildered Stephen. The principal was the laughing stock of the school and was widely considered to be a wimp by students and staff alike. Stephen, however, did not find the situation to be comical in the least. The sheer incompetence of the principal amazed Stephen. He wondered how a man of so little fortitude could be entrusted to run a large middle school. He could not understand how the principal, teachers and other staff could allow such conditions when he had seen firsthand how much differently a school could be run.

At the end of the year, Stephen's situation came to a climax when all of the students in the building were told to remain in the school gymnasium for the last two days. Stephen was not sure why all of the students were crammed into the gym in this manner, but he heard rumors that the teachers were finishing up their paperwork for the year. What Stephen did know was that there were not enough teachers in the gym to monitor the mass of bored students. At the end of the first day, a large fight broke out in the bleachers. Stephen watched in horror as one of the school system's unarmed and unequipped campus police officers attempted to intervene. The officer was quickly attacked by a group of students, overwhelmed and beaten. As the situation turned chaotic, many of the students began to flee the gym through emergency exit doors, and Stephen was forced out of the building with the crowd. Stephen later heard from friends that city police officers had been called to the school to restore order.

On the last day of school, Stephen was very concerned that there would be more violence. He decided to cut school with several of his friends to avoid potential problems. Stephen had never been truant before and had mixed feelings about his decision. Stephen and his friends roamed about until they ended up at a large discount store near the school. While the boys were looking at fishing tackle, two of them decided to shoplift some merchandise. Although Stephen did not participate in the thefts, he was in the store with them and knew of their misdeeds. As the group left the store, they were apprehended by store security personnel. The police were called, and Stephen was turned over to the responding officers along with his friends.

That summer, Stephen's father moved his family again. This time, however, he only moved to another part of the same community, to a heavily wooded and gated subdivision on a lake. Stephen liked his new home, particularly because his house sat close to the bank of the lake. He could now explore not only the woods near his home, but he could use his father's new canoe to explore the lake.

High School Hell

inally, Stephen entered high school. He found his high school to be a noticeably more orderly place than his middle school had been. One of his friends who was still attending his old middle school told him that the principal had been replaced and that the latest word was that he had been fired due to the problems at the school. Stephen was glad to be out of the chaotic environment, though his reprieve would be short-lived.

Stephen was by now a fairly withdrawn student and did not participate in many school activities. He simply wanted to get through school and go on with his life. He desperately tried to avoid problems with other students, but problems would periodically envelop him like an unwanted wet blanket.

In Stephen's senior year, violence at the school escalated. On one occasion, Stephen witnessed

a particularly vicious fight between two girls outside of the ROTC gymnasium. During the fight,
one of the girls smashed a bottle and ruthlessly
slashed her opponent. Blood was everywhere, and
the girl was badly hurt before school staff members could separate the two. Stephen was horrified at the viciousness of the assault. A few weeks
later, Stephen would hear persistent rumors that
another student had been stabbed with a pocket-
knife on a bus while it was unloading students at
the school.

Keeping up Appearances

Toward the end of his senior year, Stephen was very eager to finish school. He was literally counting the days until his "parole," as he saw it, from the school. One day, Stephen was in the ROTC gym for class. As was sometimes the case, no instructor was in the room with the students, and they were simply left to do as they pleased with general instructions such as "play volleyball" or the like. While Stephen was horsing around with one of his friends near the bleachers, someone slashed Stephen across the thigh with a box cutter. Stephen did not see who cut him, but he was sure that many of the other students did because they immediately cleared out the bleachers.

This was the last straw for Stephen. After having been criminally victimized at school on more than 100 occasions, Stephen decided to do something about it. For the first time, he decided to report the crime to school officials. He felt that the person who had attacked him must be identified and punished. He quickly proceeded to the ROTC office area and found the instructor, who was supposed to be teaching his class, reading a newspaper at his desk. When Stephen told him what had happened, the instructor did not seem very alarmed, nor did he seem concerned. He simply told Stephen to go to the main office and tell them what had happened.

Stephen went to the main office at the school and reported the incident. He was quickly hustled out of the main lobby and into a hallway near the principal's office. Several staff members gathered around him as he related the details of the incident. The staff at the school did not call his parents. They did not summon the police as Stephen had expected. They did not even call paramedics to check his injury, nor was a school nurse notified. Although the cut on Stephen's thigh was not severe, he had expected that someone would check his wound. Instead, school officials seemed interested only in how many people Stephen had told about the incident. When he informed them that he had told only the ROTC instructor, they seemed relieved.

When Stephen urged them to individually ask the students from the class who had attacked him, he was stunned by their reply. They said that questioning the students would make it more likely that the incident would be reported in the newspaper. They told him that the image of the school was important and that news reports of the incident could damage the community's view of the school. They informed Stephen that media reports of other violent incidents earlier in the year had already hurt the school's reputation and that coverage of this incident would further damage the school's image. They implored Stephen not to talk about the incident because they did not want people to think that the school was a dangerous place for students.

Stephen was dumbfounded. He now realized that the people who ran his school were the only ones on campus who did not seem to realize or care to know that it was indeed a very dangerous place for students and staff. Once Stephen realized that all they were interested in was covering up the incident, he lost what little faith and confidence he had left in the school administration. He was devastated.

Stephen became fully aware that he could not rely on the staff at the school to protect him, so he decided to take matters into his own hands. From that day forward, Stephen armed himself with more powerful weapons and a determination not to be victimized ever again. The consequences of his decision would dramatically change his life and the lives of other students and educators.

Reflections

As you have been taking this journey, it is natural that you might reflect on your own experiences as a youth. You may have recalled instances where you have been the victim of bullies. You may have even remembered occasions in which you were the bully who tormented another child or more likely, a bystander who observed such behavior. Some who will read this book may be youth who are experiencing similar victimization themselves and are trying to cope.

Adult readers who are parents may be concerned for the physical and emotional well-being of their own children as they navigate the sometimes tricky landscape faced by our children as they grow up. Others are themselves entrusted with the care of children and have been reflecting on their own roles as teachers, school administrators, scout leaders, coaches or youth volunteers.

Those of you who are entrusted with the care of your community's children may have been reevaluating the safety measures that you have in place in your organization. Those educators who are taking this journey may be wondering if there are things going on in your schools that are beyond your awareness: children being victimized or young people in dire need of assistance. For those who work in Boys and Girls Clubs facilities or the local YMCA or who coach Little League, there may be the equally important question of which of those children with whom you come into contact desperately need your help.

Whatever your situation is, my desire is to help motivate you to become even more a part of the solution to our problems with bullying, to make sure that you are a staunch advocate for the children. You see, parents, teachers, students, medical professionals, law enforcement officers, members of the faith community, political leaders, court officials, youth volunteers and countless others can all make a tremendous difference in the lives of our children. There are thousands of weakfish like Stephen who need your help right now, in your community. As Lieutenant Colonel Dave Grossman and coauthor Gloria DeGaetano point out in *Stop Teaching Our Kids to Kill – A Call To Action Against TV, Movie & Video Game Violence,* our youth have never before been so conditioned by society to commit acts of extreme violence. I hope that this journey and Stephen's story has helped you to understand what it is like for a child to grow up afraid to go to school each day, to be a prisoner of fear.

Now, surely there will be many reading this book who are already advocates for the children. Yet, here I am asking you to do even more, to give even more of yourself for the kids. Some of you are severely overworked educators who are already pushing the limits trying to meet deadlines and statistical goals that are not realistic. Others are overworked and underpaid police officers who are already risking your lives for others, and, in some cases, fighting local politics as you try to carry out your work. Some are very busy youth volunteers who somehow take time from your own families to help provide a better life for other people's children. Yet, I dare to ask even more of you.

Perhaps every reader in these situations has had one of those days. As a parent, you are busy raising your own kids, working a strenuous job, paying bills and getting the car fixed. Surely every parent has known those hectic days. Even so, now you are expected to take time to notice other people's children, volunteer or become involved with efforts to enhance the level of safety in your local schools by attending school safety task force meetings.

Perhaps, as an educator, you have had one of those Fridays from hell when you have mounds of paperwork to complete, or your school system has been criticized heavily in the media in recent weeks, often by those who have not set foot in a classroom in decades, but who think they know better how to educate the children than those with much more experience and education. Maybe you know without a doubt that you deserved that promotion that you did not get, or that the politics of education are keeping you from doing your job as well as you could. Perhaps your school is poorly funded and overcrowded, and the taxpayers do not seem the least bit concerned. Possibly, the building in which you work is in deplorable condition. You feel as if the parents don't care, many of the kids seem to care even less, and you question whether your boss or the school board members care or even understand the real issues. Then, you ask yourself if it is really all worthwhile to beat your head up against the wall trying to make a difference in the lives of these children who sometimes show blatant disrespect for others and who seem not to care about themselves or their peers.

Now there is a child outside your door, Eric, who has been so much trouble as of late, and he wants to talk to you about a problem. It is long past time to go home to see your family, to try to relax so you can be ready to take on another tough week come Monday morning. As if all that weren't more than enough, in this book you are being asked to take the extra time to pay close attention to what the boy has to say, because maybe, just maybe, what he has to say is really important. Perhaps on such occasions, you ask yourself, "Is it really worth it? Am I making a difference? Am I having an effect for all of this heartache and effort to help these kids who so often just don't seem to care?" Well, why don't we see what Stephen has to say about all of this?

Advocates

O ur journey has introduced you to many people who impacted Stephen, but there are a few people you have not yet had the opportunity, even the privilege, to meet. These are people who also had a profound impact on Stephen, every bit as powerful an impact as those boys who molested him, the barracuda that attacked him in the elementary school classroom, the thugs who robbed him in middle school or even the person who cut him in high school. In fact, as Stephen would put it, these people, these advocates for the children, had an even more profound impact than all of those who had done him harm. They would change the course of his life.

Among the people we have not yet mentioned are those dedicated teachers who, in spite of their sometimes deplorable working conditions, reached out to Stephen. One particularly remarkable educator was a high school literature teacher. She encouraged Stephen and urged him to stay on track; she told him that he had an ability to use words and that he should write. She told him to keep going his course. She, like several other teachers, had no idea of the difference she was making in his life; his ability to hang on. There were other excellent teachers as well, each making their own contributions, seemingly small, unaware of the impact of their care. There was one particular teacher who took the time to talk to his students about life skills. Another, his home room teacher in his senior year, became so concerned about the severe problem with weapons at the school that he confronted the administration about it. These and other educators were advocates for the children.

Anyone can help a child under good circumstances, but only the real advocates keep trying when the chips are down, when the odds seem insurmountable.

The leader of Stephen's Boy Scout troop ran Troop 205 with great love, care and pride. This man understood the true meaning of encouragement. He, along with his assistant scoutmasters, not only produced many Eagle Scouts, but he changed Stephen's life as well. He took his community's children camping every month. August was never too hot nor January too cold for this advocate to take time out for the children.

Stephen liked to visit two different Boys and Girls Clubs in his community. He found there dedicated men and women who took the time to help make a fun and safe place for children to play and grow, to keep them away from the dangers of the street. These advocates, too, would have an impact on the little boy.

There were also parents and law enforcement officers in Stephen's community who would have an impact on the boy. When he was taken home by an officer from the Macon Police Department after the shoplifting incident, he was given a chance to enter into a diversion program for youthful offenders. To complete the program, he joined the Macon Junior Optimist Police Program, sponsored by the Macon Police Department and the Macon Optimist Club. A committed parent volunteered her time to host meetings with the young people enrolled in the program. Even though she was perpetually busy raising her own sons, she took time with Stephen and the other children, time that would pay big dividends. There were also members of the Macon Police Department who took it upon themselves to invest time and energy into the Junior Police Optimist Program. In particular, there was an officer who dedicated much of his time to the children in the program. While other officers were out chasing "bad guys," this officer was working arduously to prevent kids from turning into criminals.

Perhaps these types of law enforcement duties are not as glamorous as chasing down an armed robbery suspect in a dark alley, but they can be just as effective in reducing crime and protecting the public.

Also, there were members of the Bibb County Sheriff's Department who were heroes for Stephen. When he was in high school, the Sheriff's Department formed a law enforcement explorer post through the Boy Scouts of America. Explorer scouts have the opportunity to interact with working professionals in various fields, including law enforcement. Through the dedication of architects, educators, medical personnel, journalists and many other professionals, exploring provides young people with a chance to learn about various careers and to talk directly with those engaged in the field. Several dedicated members of the department took time to work with the youth belonging to the post, and they too would make a difference in Stephen's life.

Through his explorer post, Stephen also had the opportunity to get to know a supervisor from the Sheriff's Department. He and his family attended Stephen's church. He on many occasions talked to Stephen about his experiences in law enforcement and about how people should be treated. In particular, he urged Stephen not only to finish high school, but to pursue a college degree.

None of these advocates had any idea what Stephen had been through. Surely, they each could tell that the boy was troubled, but they all gave much of themselves to him and impacted him far more than they could imagine. There were others who influenced the boy as well. They all made a difference in his life.

Outcomes

When Stephen finally graduated from high school, he hated school so much that he did not attend the prom, nor did he have any desire to participate in graduation ceremonies. He was simply glad to be finished with what had become for him an ordeal that had lasted more than a decade. To Stephen, school seemed to last a century. He was glad to be rid of it. He was ready to move on with his life.

Many children who have faced trials and tribulations like those experienced by Stephen have not fared well. Some have turned to illicit drugs or alcohol to numb the pain. Others have turned to a life of crime to seek revenge on a society that they feel has wronged them. Many youth drop out of school or drop out on life altogether by committing suicide in a tragic waste of precious human life. Young women and men turn to lives as prostitutes or become unwed parents when they lose respect for themselves and engage in unhealthy relationships with others who simply use them as sexual objects. As we have often seen, some victims become monsters and commit horrific acts of violence against their classmates. Each child is different and indeed unique, and we must understand that many children react differently to similar circumstances. Unless they have the support of the right advocates at the appropriate time in their lives, the outcome can be catastrophic for the child and for society.

> Fortunately, Stephen had help from the right advocates, in the right doses, at just the right moments in his life to aid him in overcoming his obstacles and his burdens. So, as an 18-year-old, Stephen, the weakfish, this frail young man, decided on the path to take. He became a police officer. Stephen had been so inspired by those who helped him he became driven to help those like him. He chose to dedicate his life to the protection of others. He did indeed work feverishly to do just that, often being told along the way by some coworkers that he worked too hard and that he cared too much for those he protected. As a police officer, he encountered many people who had done terrible things to others, those who seemed to have little regard for their fellow man. As a very aggressive young officer, he would make far more arrests than others in his department. He would always remember to treat suspects and victims alike with kindness and dignity. He would remember what one advocate had once told him – that no matter

what a suspect has done, no matter how terrible
the crime, each suspect is still a human being, and
a police officer's job is not to punish, but to bring
those who do bad things to justice. So Stephen
would carry out his duties with a passion, a relentless drive to right wrongs and to help those who
needed it.

Stephen worked hard to find those who do evil
things and bring them to justice; he worked tire-
lessly to protect and to serve others. He toiled to
reduce risk and to get help for those who needed
it. He studied his trade constantly, reading every
book, watching every training video and attending every course in his field that he could. While
at his job with a university police department, he
attended the Macon Police Academy as a guest
student for three months on his own time, without pay. He attended the basic police academy as
well and earned the trophy for best marksman as
well as the academic award for his academy class.
Stephen attended almost every class available at
the Law Enforcement Training Center of Middle
Georgia, most often on his own time, without pay,
while working his regular tours of duty. He even
took annual leave to attend the longer advanced
classes. In spite of his experiences in school, he
enrolled in college, taking advantage of the free
tuition available to all officers in the department.

On many occasions, Stephen volunteered to work on investigations during his off-duty hours without pay. Other officers sometimes scoffed at him for this, but a few others would volunteer alongside him to which reinforced his belief that his job was about the protection of people, not making over-time pay.

On one occasion, Stephen arrested a suspect who was attempting to sexually assault a coed in her apartment near the campus. The suspect matched the description of a man who had attempted to rape another student earlier in the year. Stephen and his partner volunteered to drive two hours away to Savannah, Georgia, on their off day to show a photo lineup to the victim. The chief approved their request, and they set off to Savannah.

When the task of interviewing the victim and showing her the photo spread was completed, the coed's mother began to cry. When the young officers asked what they had done to upset her, she explained that she had been raped on her way home from school when she was a child. She told them that the white police officers who had responded to the call had made light of the inci-dent, telling her that she was "just another nigger" and they did not have time to waste on such mat-ters. She had grown to hate law enforcement offi-cers over her many years and had many resentful feelings toward white people in general. She was crying because it had taken two white police officers who had used their day off to drive across the state to investigate her daughter's assault to see how things had changed. She had realized that she had in some ways become what she hated most— that she too had lumped others into one bad category because of the actions of a few.

This encounter touched Stephen and his partner Don McCown deeply. They could not imagine someone in their field being so callous, so cold-hearted, although they did know that such things had happened before. They were at once ashamed for their shields and yet proud to wear them as they represented the positive change in what was for them a noble field.

Stephen was rewarded for his hard work, for his dedication. At the age of only 19, he was promoted to corporal, and he made the rank of sergeant at the age of 21, a point when most police officers are just going to the police academy. He was promoted again to lieutenant while still just 25 years of age, a very rare occurrence in the field of law enforcement. Stephen rarely had the opportunity to supervise anyone younger than he was. After he finished his four-year degree, he began to work toward a master's degree.

Making a Difference

At the still unusually tender age of just 27 years, Stephen, the weakfish, the frail little boy who once shied so quickly from danger in any form and who had now learned to seek it out and confront it, was granted a tremendous opportunity. For Michael Stephen Dorn, the weakfish, was appointed Chief of Police for the Bibb County Public School System in Macon, Georgia, the same school system where I had been criminally victimized on well more than a hundred occasions. I was afforded a chance to change things in the district, and, with the help of many other advocates of the children, change them we would.

During the decade that I had the privilege, and indeed the honor, to serve in that capacity, the level of safety in the district became a widely emulated model for other schools around this nation and many other countries. Many school safety techniques and concepts that are now in standard usage around the country were developed by the Bibb County Campus Police Department during this time.

Working as a team in the manner described in this book, we saw student weapons violations drop by more than 90 percent and reported crimes on school property fall by more than 80 percent. We realized these reductions after we established rigid reporting requirements to make sure that we were accurately tracking and analyzing incident trends. In addition to contributing to the dramatic reductions in crime and weapons violations, officers in the department directly thwarted six planned school shootings (all gang-related), one planned school bombing and a planned double suicide by two high school students.

Furthermore, the multidisciplinary threat management model developed in Bibb County in the early 1990s is now in wide usage in various forms throughout the country. The home search technique that was developed by the department is also now a standard practice around the nation. Thousands of schools now utilize the plain view search technique that we developed to address the problem of weapons in student vehicles. We have shared these techniques with hundreds of thousands of educators, mental health professionals and law enforcement officers through articles, books, free training videos and training programs.

The techniques developed in the Bibb County Public School System have now been used to successfully thwart several dozen planned school shootings and bombings. For every school shooting rampage that you have seen reported in the news, several have been averted through the use of techniques developed in the Bibb County Public School System.

Because of the success of our program in Bibb County, I was selected as the lead technical expert for what is one of the largest government school safety centers in the country. Our unit trained more than 50,000 people in the first three years, again having a broad impact across the nation. None of these things would have happened to me, or to the many others whom I have been able to help, without the tireless efforts of my heroes, the advocates who were there for me when times were tough.

Because of the efforts of the advocates in my life, I was able to make a difference not only in my community, but in thousands of others as well. The time and energy that the advocates expended on me helped me more than I can express in words, and they helped many other children as well. Their efforts have also benefited all of the people whom I and the other recipients of their care have been able to help and influence positively.

So the next time you wonder if is worth it for you to help a child, the next time you are bullied if you are a child yourself, on the next occasion when you want to scream at the top of your lungs to the heavens above because of frustration, when you feel as if you are at the end of your rope and wonder if it is really worthwhile, think of the weakfish; think of Stephen. If your journey with Stephen and my pleas to you to give your very best effort are not enough, perhaps emergency action is required. If you are still asking yourself if it is all worthwhile, whether you can make a real difference, proceed as quickly as possible to the nearest elementary school and find a child. Perhaps you will select a second grader, maybe you will choose a little boy or possibly a little girl. If you then look into the child's eyes, you will find the answer that you seek. You may find your Stephen.

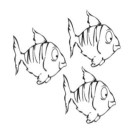

Epilogue

Our children are truly the most precious resource we have. In today's busy world we can too easily forget how difficult a journey growing up can be for our youth. The modern world is difficult not just for adults but can be hard for our children to navigate as well. Today's youth have more opportunities, but they also face many challenges that did not confront those before them to such an extent. Drugs, crime, fear of terrorism, violence in the media, deadly sexually transmitted diseases and bullying all take their toll on today's young people, who must often confront these hazards with the assistance of busy parents who cannot spend as much time with their children as they would like.

The journey outlined in *Weakfish* is designed to show how one troubled youth was able not only to survive many hurdles, but was also able to achieve and even thrive because of them. This book was written to urge readers, both young and old, to help children overcome adversity with a focus on making the world a more caring place for young people and on instilling a sense of giving back to the community along the way. We can all make a difference in the lives of young people. We can help to create a safety net to allow our children to grow and develop in a warm, caring and supportive society. All of us face many difficult challenges in our lives, and no matter what we do, children will have to bear burdens. We can, however, share the burdens and contribute in meaningful ways by striving to be advocates for the children.

The people mentioned in this book who made such a difference in my life focused much on giving to others. They relieved me of many heavy burdens and prepared me to pass their kindness and generosity to others. They truly planted shade trees of goodwill to benefit future generations as they clearly also helped many other children with their great deeds. There are many thousands more unsung heroes who are capable and willing advocates for the children. I urge any young person who is having a tough time of it to actively seek out the advocates who can help them.

Help often comes in the strangest forms. I have often heard people who work with children speak negatively of the use of arrest as a means to address problems with youth. The phrase, "We don't want to ruin their life by giving them a criminal record" has been used time and time again with genuine concern by those who work with youth. I hasten to point out that had I not been arrested as a youth, I would never have become a police officer, let alone a police chief. Had this intervention not taken place, I would never have received my required appointment from the Director of the FBI to attend the FBI National Academy program receiving three months of some of the best training available to any officer, and I surely would not have had the opportunity to train with my colleagues in New York City, Israel and many other places. In fact, no one knows how my life might have turned out had I not taken that ride in a patrol car to begin my metamorphosis into a law enforcement officer. I do know that my life is better because of that ride. Sometimes support is what our children need, and sometimes it is the tough love of consequences for their less appropriate actions. I had the good fortune to receive both that day.

I love to explore the world now as much as I did when I was a little boy playing in the woods near my home in Buffalo, New York. My work has allowed me to snorkel in the Red Sea, wander in Glacier National Park and visit the splendor of nature in Oregon and other wonderful places around the world too numerous to mention. As with many of my other books, the first draft of this manuscript was written in a beautiful cabin nestled in the North Georgia mountains, with the alluring and relaxing sounds of a babbling trout stream distracting me from time to time as I collected my thoughts in this peaceful retreat.

My experiences have allowed me much time to get to know my own precious son, who also travels the country teaching others how better to protect children. Our trips together mean more to me than any material possession I could ever own. In spite of the painful experiences that I endured as a child, I have been truly blessed as an adult and as a father.

In this book, I have discussed many situations where children suffered because of the shortcomings of adults. I have been critical of others for these faults. In fairness, I should point out that schools and other organizations can and do frequently make dramatic comebacks from these situations as well. Many of the schools and communities mentioned here have implemented excellent safety programs, and much progress has been made.

As but one example, I should point out that my son chose to attend the same high school that I attended, and he did so as a magnet student in the International Baccalaureate program. Even though the building has aged much and the neighborhood surrounding the school has declined even more, the school has improved markedly. My son had a great time attending his senior prom, and I was as proud as any parent has ever been to watch him cross the stage to receive his diploma. Through the support of many fine educators in the Bibb County Public School System, my son scored incredibly well on the Scholastic Aptitude Test and started college at Georgia Institute of Technology this fall. He made me proud when he announced his intention to protect and serve his fellow man as a police officer after college. My son and I are very close and openly discuss many issues, and my son assures me that he has never been afraid to use the rest room in a Bibb County public school. Oh, how things have changed.

Practical Solutions

Advice for Educators

Educators who do not make bullying a priority are playing a dangerous game of Russian roulette. First, they are risking the lives of students. They are risking the lives of those who are being bullied, those who are exhibiting bullying behaviors and the rest of the student body.

There have been cases where victims of bullying have committed suicide or bullies have killed their victims because school officials did not intervene properly. For example, in one Georgia case, a school district was involved in litigation over an incident where a chronically bullied child committed suicide with a handgun during class. Yet the district was again shocked when another tragedy occurred after a child repeatedly attacked other children. After several dozen such attacks occurred without proper intervention, the aggressive child attacked a smaller youth he had been bullying. The attack resulted in the victim going into a coma, and he died when he was taken off of life support. In other rare cases, bullied children have used weapons to kill and injure students who bullied them. In some unusually rare examples of these cases, children have committed multiple victim weapons assaults. In at least one of these cases, the victimized student was so enraged that he took great pains while planning his attack to make sure he would be able to kill the principal of his school. His feeling was that the principal was ultimately responsible for the environment at the school and thus, the horrible treatment he received there. He did indeed murder the school's principal during his attack.

There is another negative outcome for school officials who do not make bullying prevention and intervention a priority. There is an increasing trend for severely bullied students to seek redress through the court system. There have been a number of civil suits against school systems, and in particular against school principals, involving allegations that severe bullying was not properly addressed. Many of these cases are successful, and the trend in school violence related suits is one of high payouts if the plaintiff wins. I would be surprised if the number of bullying related lawsuits against school officials does not increase significantly because of these cases, and this type of suit may become relatively commonplace in the next decade. For this reason, school systems and school administrators should be thorough in not only addressing bullying situations, but in carefully documenting their actions to resolve them as well.

Some states have taken a progressive approach to bullying at the state level. Georgia, Indiana, North Carolina and a number of other states have passed state laws requiring school systems to create comprehensive bullying policies and to address bullying in specific ways. Sadly, many of these laws were passed in the wake of murders and suicides of school children who were victims of bullying. We advise our school clients to enact specific bullying policies which clearly define bullying behaviors, require specific action by school employees and state meaningful consequences for those who bully.

Unfortunately, there have been those who advocate that punishment is ineffective in resolving bullying situations. Children have died because of this dangerous assertion. While consequences will not prevent and resolve bullying situations alone, no bullying program will prove to be effective without meaningful consequences for those who victimize others. One student who was physically assaulted on numerous occasions in a school that lacked serious consequences for bullying behaviors of a criminal nature (such as physical assault) brought a handgun to school and opened fire in a crowded middle school hallway, killing one student and wounding others. The student reported the assaults to the school's administration and even walked into the local police station and requested that his assailants be arrested. No charges were filed. After the shooting, the student was acquitted by a jury of murder and aggravated assault charges. Jurors were sympathetic to the child who repeatedly attempted to resolve the situation through the courts only to be ignored by school and police officials. I believe strongly that the topic of consequences for the actions of bullies and for educators who do not properly address bullying in their schools has been ineffectively addressed up to this point.

My personal experiences include instances where hundreds of educators patently ignored and even covered up serious and obvious bullying behaviors. I also saw this in calls I received from exasperated parents when I worked as Georgia's School Safety Specialist. From their calls, it is clear to me that there have been and still are educators who are absolutely unfit to have responsibility for children. Just as there are corrupt police officials, incompetent doctors and others who should be removed from their positions, there are educators who are not competent to work with our precious and malleable youth. Some of the most callous human behaviors I witnessed in my 25 years of public service as a police officer and a government school safety expert involved educators who doomed children to deplorable existences and in some cases horrible deaths through their lack of action. The elementary through high school years can be crucial turning points for many students, to the point of deciding whether the child will have a successful life and future or become a dropout, drug addict or the like. Those who treated Stephen in such a cruel manner are fortunate that he did not know then that he could have not only filed criminal charges for their actions in covering up his victimization, but that he could have surely taken most of their personal wealth through litigation. While this may seem harsh, readers should understand that their actions were more harmful to Stephen than the actual victimizations that they allowed to occur while they were being paid a salary to perform a job they chose - a job which above all else involved protecting children. The fact that at least in one case, they were more concerned about the public image of their school than the safety of the children in it is still more disturbing to Stephen than the acts of the teenagers who sexually molested him.

Fortunately, there are more educators today that understand how the consistent enforcement of bullying policies and criminal laws is just as important as consistency in efforts to support victims and those who bully them. Effective bullying programs should use a comprehensive approach that involves all aspects of the school community. Efforts to educate students, parents and school staff are critical to an environment where bullying is the exception rather than the rule. While it is important to address the needs of students who are bullied and those who regularly bully others, the research of Dan Olweus and other top experts demonstrates that changing the attitudes of other students, parents and educators is required to achieve maximum benefit. Of particular note is the fact that peer mediation programs, while valuable in other ways, are not an appropriate tool for bullying situations. Bullying is not a conflict between two students, but an abuse of power by those who are (at least) perceived to be more powerful than others. Using peer mediation to address bullying is like forcing the victim of a crime to sit in a room with the person who attacked them to work things out with a moderator. Peer mediation is not only ineffective in this case, but can be extremely counterproductive to resolve bullying in schools.

Another area that has often been neglected is the physical climate of schools in relation to bullying. Setting a positive, caring and supportive climate where supervision of students is more effective can be a powerful tool to aid other efforts to effectively address bullying. In addition, we find the physical assessment of schools can help identify specific locations where bullying is taking place due to inadequate supervision. Particularly when combined with student, staff and parent surveys, this type of assessment can be incredibly effective. We developed our bullying site survey training programs and our free Web site tutorials from our tactical site survey train-the-trainer program. The tactical site survey train-the-trainer program was developed for the Indiana School Safety Specialist Academy. Clarissa Snapp, the Academy's Executive Director, became concerned when a school safety consultant charged an Indiana district $45,000 to conduct safety audits at three small schools. For less than the consultant charged to survey three schools, we can modify one of our train-the-trainer programs so representatives from every Indiana school corporation can be trained to conduct their own tactical site surveys. Internally conducted tactical site surveys are not only less expensive than those conducted by private consultants, but are often more effective as well. In addition, using local personnel to conduct tactical site surveys helps to affect a greater cultural change in schools. When school staff is heavily involved in the site survey process, staff begin to incorporate safety into daily routines to a much higher degree. These trainees can in turn train others in their school systems to conduct tactical site surveys year after year with a license to utilize our training materials. The Council for Leaders in Alabama Schools retained Safe Havens to develop a series of anti-bullying workshops, which include a physical bullying site survey process for Alabama educators. Feedback from educators around the country indicates at least a perception that this approach not only reduces safety problems like bullying, but will help to improve academic performance. As one school administrator who attended the training in Helena, Montana put it, he thought his school had done everything they knew to do to raise test scores until he realized that creating a safety culture through this process would make his school a more pleasant and welcoming place. Like Les Nichols, Vice President of Boys and Girls Clubs of America, he feels strongly that a fun and safe place is also a more effective place for children to learn.

We suggest that every private school and public school system should adopt a research - based anti-bullying program, such as the one that is available to them at no cost through the federal government (www.StopBullyingNow.hrsa.gov). On a personal level, educators should see bullying for what it is -- a serious threat to the children they serve, their school and to themselves. As with other crucial safety measures, failure to adequately protect the children of others can be one of those deal breakers in an educator's career. Some educators have found themselves out of work when bad things happened to good kids due to their negligence. No educator wants to bear this financial burden in addition to the emotional burden they will undoubtedly experience when a child dies because they did not do their job.

Advice for School Resource Officers

According to a statewide survey conducted in Florida a few years ago, Florida high school students identified their school resource officer as the most trusted adult on campus. As the survey had no connection to any police organization, many people including school resource officers were surprised that more than 90 percent of Florida high school students felt this way. This indicates how likely it is for a school resource officer to be in a position to assist children who are bullied. This also shows why many students seek out the school resource officer rather than those we would more traditionally think students would turn to for bullying problems.

The school resource officer can have a profound effect on bullying in a school. For example, it is common for students who are the victims of criminal bullying to lose faith in school officials who fail to treat criminal acts as crimes simply because they occur on school property. The student often cannot understand why it is suddenly not a criminal offense only because they were victimized at school. The case where the student was acquitted of murder and aggravated assault in a Georgia middle school is a case in point of the desperation a child can feel when abandoned by adults who fail to treat crimes as crimes when they happen at school. In this case, not only did school officials fail to do their job and let a child down, but the police failed to perform their duties as well with devastating results for the child, innocent bystanders, the school and the community.

This is one challenge faced by the school resource officer: Making school officials, students, parents, court officials and their peers and supervisors understand that certain types of bullying behaviors are also crimes. When a student is beaten up, jammed into a locker and locked inside, criminal acts have taken place. In the state of Georgia, this crime is actually a felony kidnapping, yet such incidents were covered up by school officials in that state. Part of the school resource officer's job is to bring those who commit crimes to justice and no one needs to see this more than the chronically bullied child. If the police allow a child to be criminally victimized without the consequence of the law, the child will lose faith in the police, our system of justice and often, faith in adults.

At the same time, the school resource officer must remember to interact in a positive fashion with school administrators, parents, other involved students and other experts like mental health professionals and school nurses who may be able to provide valuable assistance to the chronically bullied child. While some in law enforcement would scoff at the previous information, dismissing bullying as trivial compared to the serious crime in our communities and "real police work", a broader vision reveals the importance of the very real police work entailed in bullying reduction. A significant percentage of the serious offenders officers deal with regularly bullied others in school without consequence, which led them down a path to prison. We also know that many of the students who drop out of school and fill our prisons are dyslexic. How many of these inmates dropped out because of the high rate of school victimization of dyslexic children? Bullying reduction is not only important police work from the standpoint of protecting the victims. The data indicate it may be an effective means for officers to help protect society from criminals by diverting high-risk youth from a life of crime.

Advice for School Mental Health Professionals

School mental health professionals play several key roles in addressing the significant problems of bullying in schools. Often, alert school mental health professionals spot indications that a child is being tormented at school and can get the child to open up about the problem. In other instances, students who have been bullied or who have bullied other children are referred to school mental health personnel. In either situation, the dedicated mental health professional can make a significant difference with patience, perseverance and creativity.

When a school mental health professional learns that a child was bullied, it is important for them to remember that bullied children, like victims of sexual assault are often reluctant to provide all relevant details and often do not report the most serious victimizations they experienced. Like a rape victim, the chronically bullied child may be embarrassed or afraid to relate all aspects of their victimization. The mental health professional must gently develop trust and a solid rapport with the child to ensure the full extent of the bullying is revealed and to best help the child cope. Of course, the mental health professional will often need to provide mental health services to aid the bullied child in coping with the pain, suffering and embarrassment that often accompany their situation.

Just as important as assistance to the bullied child, mental health professionals are often called upon to speak with the child who is caught bullying other children. The foremost consideration in these situations is that consequences be blended with any other approach. The research shows that children who frequently bully do not have a well-developed sense of empathy for their victims and often do not believe their actions cause any real pain or harm.

Helping them understand this may prove beneficial, and demonstrating the severity of their harm through significant consequences may help. In addition, the victim and other children need to see consequences for those who bully others. While discipline should be private, the reality is that the child who is disciplined most often tells others about their punishment, which can reinforce to other children the school's intolerance for such behavior.

Advice for School Nurses

School nurses are key resources that unfortunately are often overlooked in school safety initiatives. But they are valuable allies in efforts to combat bullying. Already predisposed to remain alert to signs of child abuse in children they see, school nurses often uncover bullying cases. As with the other practitioners in this section, the school nurse should be prepared to build a rapport with a child when bullying is suspected. The bullied child will frequently explain away suspicious injuries and must trust any adult before revealing what has really happened to them. This major step can be made easy by a caring and supportive demeanor though many cases will require gentle persistence on the part of the nurse.

Another difficult hurdle can be persuading the child who has made a painful disclosure to speak with other adults, such as a school administrator or school resource officer. This situation can be compounded when the professional who must be notified has a reputation for being lax in discipline or commitment. I have had many school nurses tell me horror stories about administrators in their schools who work so hard to downplay problems that they will dissuade a child who makes a report after confiding in the school nurse. As with the school resource officer or any other professional, there are times when the school nurse will need to push an administrator who is not dealing with a serious bullying case. In many instances, it may be the parent of the child who is in the best position to push the issue when confronted by an administrator who is not taking a bullying case seriously.

Advice For Students Who Are Being Bullied

Advice for students who are being bullied or who witness bullying is a little more elusive. Unfortunately, victims of bullying have somewhat limited power to affect the outcome of their situation. Unless they are forced by an unusually difficult situation to retain an attorney and take legal action, they are often reliant upon parents, educators, law enforcement officers and other students for support in chronic bullying situations. There are many varying situations that require different strategies to resolve. There are no one-size-fits-all solutions. There are, however, some actions that students can take to reduce the chances that bullying will continue.

Generally speaking, a student who is being bullied should seek out an adult they respect and trust and ask for assistance. This may be a parent, a teacher, a school administrator, a school resource officer, Girl Scout or Boy Scout leader, counselor or other adult. When seeking help from an adult, it is important that they give an accurate and complete description of the situation. Often, students have difficulty talking to others about bullying victimization. This is a natural response to a personal and often painful situation. But telling an adult only part of what bullying problems occurred makes it hard for them to provide reliable advice.

Mature and trusted friends may also be helpful. While it is typically more helpful to approach an adult, responsible friends may be able to offer some advice and support. In many cases, a friend may be willing to assist another student in approaching a responsible adult. In other cases, the moral support they offer may be helpful.

Some potential courses of action that at times have proven to be helpful in reducing problems include:

- Closer supervision by school staff/bus drivers

- Rescheduling a bully's class schedule

- Suspension of the bully

- Prosecution of the bully

- Requesting that one or more bullies be reassigned to another school or ordered to stay away from you

- Other approaches have typically proven to make the situation worse.

Do not:

- Join a gang

- Assault a bully

- Carry or use a weapon

All of the above will lead to more harm than good, and you will no longer have the moral (or legal) high ground. Being bullied at school is bad, but the level of victimization you may experience in a detention facility is almost assuredly going to be far worse.

Advice for Parents

As with students, it can be difficult to provide appropriate advice to parents whose children are victims of bullying. First and foremost, I would urge any parent who learns that their child is being bullied to ask questions and listen intently. Remember that bullied children, particularly those who are chronically bullied, are often reluctant to talk about their experiences. You may have to gently pull the information from the child with patient understanding. Be sure that you have a good idea of what the child has been experiencing before dispensing advice.

Seek your child's permission to talk to staff and the school. Talking with administrators, teachers, school resource officers, bus drivers and other staff can be effective. Unfortunately, many parents have told me that they talked with staff from their child's school and school system only to be rebuffed with inaction and excuses. Having served in a school district for ten years, I would point out that every school employee has a supervisor. Even school superintendents and private school headmasters are accountable to a board. I would urge parents to try to work with school officials whenever possible. I also tell them to avail themselves of the chain of command in the educational organization if necessary. I also point out to parents that it may be appropriate to notify the police of some bullying situations, particularly those involving physical violence among middle and high school students. In the federally funded bullying prevention program listed in the resqurce section, parents are also told to consider availing themselves of legal counsel in severe cases when school officials will not take appropriate action. I think we are going to see far more parents choose this course of action in the future.

Perhaps the most important thing parents of a bullied child can do is to support their child at all costs. I agree with Dr, James Dobson who advises parents that they should never leave a child in a school where they are being bullied. If the school cannot find a way to resolve the situation, it may be necessary to take the child out of the dangerous environment. Though it is unfair to make the child suffer rather than those who are causing the problem, it may be preferable to move the child to a safer environment.

School Assessment Instruments

Previously, the most effective research-based bullying programs have incorporated two types of assessment tools to help school officials determine the extent of bullying and the times, situations and locations where bullying occurs. The first type of tool is used to assess the reported level of bullying and bullying related incidents. This approach involves a careful review and analysis of reported incident data. The second approach involves the evaluation of unreported incidents of bullying and bullying behaviors and the manner in which staff and students respond to bullying in the school. These two approaches are the most crucial first steps to reduce bullying in our schools. Until and unless school officials use a systematic approach to evaluate the level of bullying behaviors, the times, situations and locations where bullying is most often occurring and the manner in which students and staff respond to bullying situations, they are absolutely guessing as to the extent of bullying in their schools. As we have seen, this type of uneducated guessing has disastrous results for many schools and children.

There is a third type of assessment tool not traditionally applied to help school officials determine the extent and location of bullying in schools. The two types of physical assessments – the Tactical Site Survey and the Student School Climate Facility Site Survey — can dramatically improve the level and quality of supervision of students in a school while creating a warmer climate that is more conducive to learning. The author conducts Tactical Site Survey Training Sessions for school districts and at state and national conferences. Some state school safety centers, such as those in Indiana and Georgia, offer free training and technical assistance in coordinating or training for tactical site surveys. A detailed tactical site survey template is available at no cost on the Safe Havens International Inc. web site at *www.weakfish.org/resources.html.*

School officials should conduct their own tactical site surveys rather than contracting with private for fee consultants. The majority of school safety consultants do not have professional qualifications to perform tactical site surveys that are any better than those that can be conducted by properly trained school administrators. Just as importantly, the tactical site survey process is designed to cause a permanent cultural change because school staff naturally ingrain safety into their daily routine. For example, it is common for a fire service professional to conduct an annual fire inspection at a school and to note numerous code violations in their report. Hopefully, these hazards are immediately corrected, but typically, similar hazards are found the next year because the inspection process does not change the behavior of school officials because they are not part of the evaluation process. When school officials are properly trained on how to conduct a tactical site survey and coordinate the survey with local law enforcement, fire, emergency management and other officials, the process becomes an interactive effort. Thereafter they view their building quite differently, which changes their behavior in a positive way. Instead of reacting to hazards that are found once each year, they begin to take corrective action on a daily basis. They also begin to more effectively influence staff to not create or allow hazardous situations, such as blocking a fire exit doors with a trashcan or leaving an unoccupied classroom unlocked (creating an opportunity for negligent privacy). This is another reason why it can be less effective to use consultants to coordinate site surveys.

The Tactical Site Survey

The physical design of a school can contribute to an environment that is more conducive to bullying. The manner in which a school facility is used can also increase or lessen the likelihood of bullying. The author's training programs and conference presentations on bullying site surveys are extremely popular. This process allows educators and community partners to design schools with a warmer climate and increase the level of supervision dramatically. Likewise, educators have reported positive results after the application of this process to existing buildings. Our complete 20-page tactical site survey checklist can be obtained for free at our Web site at *www.weakfish.org/resources.html*. The checklist can be simply downloaded and used in printed form or used electronically. In electronic format, the checklist has general consideration sections that expand automatically so detailed comments and recommendations can be included.

The tactical site survey will also help to dramatically reduce the risk of violence, accidents, fire and other situations that can lead to death, injury and damage to property. Some school administrators have said that they do not have the time to conduct a tactical site survey once each year and either do not conduct them or waste money hiring school safety consultants to do what can be done as well, and in most cases better, by properly trained school officials. From a time management standpoint, it is inefficient for an administrator to not take the one day a year that is required to conduct a tactical site survey of their school. One safety incident that could easily be prevented through this process can and often does consume more time than the time devoted to a decade's worth of site surveys. In addition, this process can reduce civil liability, reduce maintenance costs, help to improve test scores and save lives. A building principal who does not coordinate a tactical site survey at their school each year is failing to perform one of the most basic, inexpensive and important safety measures available to them, and their school is as a result, not as safe as it could and should be. Reading a report generated by a consultant is not as revealing as seeing the hazards firsthand while participating in the site survey.

Student School Climate Facility Site Survey

Another beneficial approach is to enlist the assistance of students in conducting physical assessments of their schools to help administrators identify and correct vulnerabilities that can contribute to bullying and other safety hazards. The Student School Climate Facility Survey is a more condensed instrument than the Tactical Site Survey Template and is designed to fit within a student's perspective. This process can be extremely revealing for those school officials who wish to seek out and correct hazards, rather than find out through a homicide or suicide that there are significant problems in their school. Safe Havens International has a short and simple tutorial program on the above listed Web site that will help students learn how to spot a variety of situations that can make their school more dangerous. This template is designed for use by a team of students accompanied by at least one school staff member. Upon completion of the survey, the site survey form should be given to the principal of the school.

Tactical Site Survey

Date of Evaluation:

Date of Survey:

Surveyors:

Staff/faculty member guiding student assessment team:

Name of Facility:

Name of School System:

Address of Facility:

SCHOOL SAFETY ZONE CONSIDERATIONS:

Please list any concerns for student safety in the neighborhood 1,000 feet in all directions from the school.

1.

FACILITY CONSIDERATIONS:

Please list any general concerns about the school facility itself.

1.

OTHER COMMENTS/CONSIDERATIONS:

_____

_____

_____

_____

_____

_____

_____

_____

_____

_____

PERIMITER AND SCHOOL SAFETY ZONE

	N/A	Adequate	Please consider further	Comments	Follow-up Activities
Is visitor directional signage easy to read and understand?					
Is the school clearly marked in a manner that builds pride of students, staff and parents (murals, mascots or other identifiers)?					
Are visitor parking areas easily observed from the school?					
Is there good natural surveillance of the front entrance from the street?					
Are shrubs and trees at the entrance properly trimmed to enhance natural surveillance?					
Are students prohibited from congregating in unsupervised groups off but near campus in the mornings, at lunch or in the afternoon?					
Are there signs that students have been smoking close to campus?					

	N/A	Adequate	Please consider further	Comments	Follow-up Activities
Are there hiding areas near campus where students gather without being observed?					

SCHOOL GROUNDS

	N/A	Adequate	Please consider further	Comments	Follow-up Activities
Are unsupervised students observed on campus?					
Are areas where students can congregate in the morning, during lunch and at the end of the school day clearly designated and enforced?					
Are there any areas where unsupervised students are gathered in the morning, during lunch and in the afternoon?					
Are bushes and trees trimmed to minimize hiding places?					
Is the presence of graffiti on walls/outbuildings observed?					

SCHOOL GROUNDS (continued)

	N/A	Adequate	Please consider further	Comments	Follow-up Activities
Are there designated after hour student pick-up areas that are supervised by school staff?					
Are there cigarette butts on the ground in certain areas indicating that students are smoking on campus and therefore not being properly supervised?					
Is trash on the ground a common site indicating a lack of pride/ownership in the school?					
Are there areas where it is easy for someone to hide because of blind spots created by trees or shrubbery?					
Are school staff noticeably present in all areas of the campus where students are allowed during the morning, lunch, class change periods and in the afternoon?					
Can profanity be heard while walking around the school?					

	N/A	Adequate	Please consider further	Comments	Follow-up Activities
Can verbal abuse, demeaning words, put downs or other bullying behaviors be heard while walking the campus?					

SCHOOL FACILITY

Hallways and Main Areas:

Yes	No	Are there directional signs that are easy to understand?
Yes	No	Are unused lockers secured so that students cannot be locked inside by bullies?
Yes	No	Does each hallway have adequate clearance for the number of students, making it easier for teachers and staff to observe students and harder for students to get trapped in crowded hallways by bullies?
Yes	No	Would designation of one-way hallways and/or stairwells make it easier for students to change classes and for staff to observe students during class changes?
Yes	No	Are all hallways clear of vending machines, coat racks/ and other items that block visibility of school staff?
Yes	No	If surveillance cameras are present, do they appear to cover areas outside bathrooms and in blind spots such as stairwells?
Yes	No	If shaded bubble protectors are used for cameras, are they clean?
Yes	No	Is no profanity heard while walking around the school?
Yes	No	Are no verbal abuse, demeaning words, put downs or other bullying behaviors heard while walking the campus?
Yes	No	Is school staff noticeably present in all areas of the campus where students are allowed during the morning, lunch, class change periods and in the afternoon?

SCHOOL FACILITY

Hallways and Main Areas (continued):

Yes	No	Is the inside of the building and are areas around the building free of cigarette butts? (These would indicate a lack of adequate supervision of the area before, during or after school)

Media Center

Yes	No	Are the bookshelves oriented so media center staff can easily see between stacks?
Yes	No	Are surveillance mirrors present in room corners to assist in supervision around bookcases?
Yes	No	Are computer screens facing in the same direction so staff can easily monitor computer activity?
Yes	No	Do computer filter programs block terrorist and hate group Web sites?

Cafeteria:

Yes	No	Are all of the following secured and monitored: any lockable cabinets, rooms or storage containers large enough for a student to be locked inside by bullies?
Yes	No	Are teachers and other staff stationed in different areas of the cafeteria so they can adequately supervise students in every section of the cafeteria?
Yes	No	Are objects blocking the view of parts of the room occupied by students moved to permit better supervision?
Yes	No	Are there security cameras in the cafeteria?

Gymnasium:

Yes	No	
Yes	No	Are all of the following secured and monitored: any lockable cabinets, rooms or storage containers large enough for a student to be locked inside by bullies?
Yes	No	Are coaches and other staff who supervise students close enough to hear and see bullying of students?
Yes	No	Are the retractable bleachers locked on a daily basis?
Yes	No	Are the areas behind bleachers supervised or secured so that students cannot be in areas out of view of staff?

Walking the Perimeter:

Yes	No	
Yes	No	All unused exterior buildings secured?
Yes	No	Is there video surveillance outside?
Yes	No	Do exterior doors remain locked throughout the day?
Yes	No	Are all exterior doors to the facility secure with the exception of the main entrance adjacent to the office area?
Yes	No	Is graffiti removed expeditiously?

Athletic Fields and Playgrounds:

Yes	No	
Yes	No	Do teachers carry a walkie-talkie when they are using the recreation facilities?
Yes	No	Are teachers who supervise students close enough to hear and see bullying of students?

Policy, Procedure, custom or practice:

Yes	No	Does the school have a bullying policy that is well known among students?
Yes	No	Does the policy have clear consequences for violators?
Yes	No	Are police/school resource officers notified if a student is physically assaulted?

SCHOOL FACILITY

Policy, Procedure, custom or practice (continued):

Yes	No	Does the school have a bullying policy that is well known among students?
Yes	No	Does the school have at least one School Resource Officer or Campus Police Officer?
Yes	No	Does the school clearly notify all students to report anyone who makes threatening statements?
Yes	No	Does the school clearly notify all students of several different options they have to report threatening statements and situations?
Yes	No	Does the school clearly describe the types of threatening statements that should be reported?
Yes	No	Is there an anonymous reporting box in an area that is not well-traveled in your facility to allow students to report possible policy and criminal violations occurring on school grounds while maintaining their anonymity?
Yes	No	Are students clearly advised of counseling services that are available to students experiencing difficulty?
Yes	No	Are formal groups in the school allowed to engage in bullying or taunting behavior towards other students (such as athletic, academic and other teams)?
Yes	No	Are informal groups in the school allowed to have participants that seem to exclude, taunt or bully some students (such as affluent students, groups of students of the same race, etc.)?

School Climate Surveys

School officials cannot accurately gauge the level of safety and bullying without surveys of students staff and parents. The following surveys are designed to help accurately evaluate safety at a school and to elicit useful suggestions from students, staff and parents. Surveys should be utilized once each year and the results used to drive prevention efforts such as improved supervision, development of new safety procedures and the purchase of safety equipment such as surveillance cameras. Teachers should assist students on parts of the survey that involve concepts that are difficult for younger students to understand, such as racism and bigotry.

Elementary Student Survey

What is the name of your school?	
Are you a boy or a girl?	
What grade are you in?	
How old are you?	
How long have you been at this school?	
How do you get to school each day?	

Please circle the answer that shows how you feel					
My school is a clean place.	Strongly Agree	Agree	Neutral	Disagree	Strongly Disagree
I have friends at this school.	Strongly Agree	Agree	Neutral	Disagree	Strongly Disagree

Students don't argue very much at this school.	Strongly Agree	Agree	Neutral	Disagree	Strongly Disagree
Students rarely fight at this school.	Strongly Agree	Agree	Neutral	Disagree	Strongly Disagree
I like this school.	Strongly Agree	Agree	Neutral	Disagree	Strongly Disagree
Students are rarely beaten up by other students.	Strongly Agree	Agree	Neutral	Disagree	Strongly Disagree
Students do not pick on, call names, or tease other students at this school.	Strongly Agree	Agree	Neutral	Disagree	Strongly Disagree
I have not had anything of mine stolen at school this year.	Strongly Agree	Agree	Neutral	Disagree	Strongly Disagree
I feel safe at school.	Strongly Agree	Agree	Neutral	Disagree	Strongly Disagree
School is a fun place.	Strongly Agree	Agree	Neutral	Disagree	Strongly Disagree
I feel safe in the lunchroom.	Strongly Agree	Agree	Neutral	Disagree	Strongly Disagree
I feel safe in the school hallways.	Strongly Agree	Agree	Neutral	Disagree	Strongly Disagree
I feel safe in the bathrooms.	Strongly Agree	Agree	Neutral	Disagree	Strongly Disagree
I feel safe in the classrooms.	Strongly Agree	Agree	Neutral	Disagree	Strongly Disagree
I feel safe at the school playground.	Strongly Agree	Agree	Neutral	Disagree	Strongly Disagree
I feel safe going to and from school.	Strongly Agree	Agree	Neutral	Disagree	Strongly Disagree
Troublemakers should be suspended or expelled.	Strongly Agree	Agree	Neutral	Disagree	Strongly Disagree
Students don't get away with too much.	Strongly Agree	Agree	Neutral	Disagree	Strongly Disagree

Students know what behavior is expected of them.	Strongly Agree	Agree	Neutral	Disagree	Strongly Disagree
Teachers enforce the rules when something bad happens.	Strongly Agree	Agree	Neutral	Disagree	Strongly Disagree
Teachers listen to me when I have a problem.	Strongly Agree	Agree	Neutral	Disagree	Strongly Disagree
I can depend on my teachers to keep my school safe.	Strongly Agree	Agree	Neutral	Disagree	Strongly Disagree
Teachers enjoy teaching here.	Strongly Agree	Agree	Neutral	Disagree	Strongly Disagree
The rules for punishing students are fair.	Strongly Agree	Agree	Neutral	Disagree	Strongly Disagree
Principals are fair with discipline.	Strongly Agree	Agree	Neutral	Disagree	Strongly Disagree
My school holds fire drills once per month.	Strongly Agree	Agree	Neutral	Disagree	Strongly Disagree
My school holds drills on emergencies, other than fire drills, twice per school year.	Strongly Agree	Agree	Neutral	Disagree	Strongly Disagree
My school is prepared for any emergency.	Strongly Agree	Agree	Neutral	Disagree	Strongly Disagree
My school provides guidance and counseling services I need.	Strongly Agree	Agree	Neutral	Disagree	Strongly Disagree
Other students enjoy learning.	Strongly Agree	Agree	Neutral	Disagree	Strongly Disagree
I am learning a lot in school.	Strongly Agree	Agree	Neutral	Disagree	Strongly Disagree
Doing well in school is important.	Strongly Agree	Agree	Neutral	Disagree	Strongly Disagree
My school is doing a good job.	Strongly Agree	Agree	Neutral	Disagree	Strongly Disagree
I am proud of this school.	Strongly Agree	Agree	Neutral	Disagree	Strongly Disagree

During this school year, how many times have YOU experienced and/or witnessed the following problems in your school?					
Verbal threats in school	Never	One Time This Year	One Time Per Month	One Time Per Week	Daily
Physical violence in school	Never	One Time This Year	One Time Per Month	One Time Per Week	Daily
Students with weapons in school	Never	One Time This Year	One Time Per Month	One Time Per Week	Daily
Students with drugs or alcohol in school	Never	One Time This Year	One Time Per Month	One Time Per Week	Daily
Drugs sold in school	Never	One Time This Year	One Time Per Month	One Time Per Week	Daily
Teasing or bullying in school	Never	One Time This Year	One Time Per Month	One Time Per Week	Daily
Gang activity in school	Never	One Time This Year	One Time Per Month	One Time Per Week	Daily
Stealing in school	Never	One Time This Year	One Time Per Month	One Time Per Week	Daily
Vandalism of school property	Never	One Time This Year	One Time Per Month	One Time Per Week	Daily
Discrimination or racism at school	Never	One Time This Year	One Time Per Month	One Time Per Week	Daily
Violence in the community around the school	Never	One Time This Year	One Time Per Month	One Time Per Week	Daily
Cheating on homework or tests	Never	One Time This Year	One Time Per Month	One Time Per Week	Daily

Comments:

Please write any additional comments on the following page. Please list any places where you feel unsafe at school or on the way to school. What could your teachers and principal do to make school feel safer?

Secondary Student Survey

What is the name of your school?	
Are you male or female?	
What is your grade level?	
How old are you?	
How long have you been at this school?	
How do you typically get to school?	

Please circle the answer that most applies to YOUR experiences this school year.					
My school is generally clean.	Strongly Agree	Agree	Neutral	Disagree	Strongly Disagree
I have made friends at this school.	Strongly Agree	Agree	Neutral	Disagree	Strongly Disagree
Arguments among students in school are rare.	Strongly Agree	Agree	Neutral	Disagree	Strongly Disagree
Fights among students are rare at school.	Strongly Agree	Agree	Neutral	Disagree	Strongly Disagree
Threats by students against one another are rare.	Strongly Agree	Agree	Neutral	Disagree	Strongly Disagree
Students are rarely beaten up by other students.	Strongly Agree	Agree	Neutral	Disagree	Strongly Disagree
Students are rarely picked on, called names, or teased by other students.	Strongly Agree	Agree	Neutral	Disagree	Strongly Disagree
I have not had anything of mine stolen at school this year.	Strongly Agree	Agree	Neutral	Disagree	Strongly Disagree
I generally feel safe at school.	Strongly Agree	Agree	Neutral	Disagree	Strongly Disagree
I feel safe on school grounds before school.	Strongly Agree	Agree	Neutral	Disagree	Strongly Disagree
I feel safe on school grounds after school.	Strongly Agree	Agree	Neutral	Disagree	Strongly Disagree
I feel safe in the school lunchroom.	Strongly Agree	Agree	Neutral	Disagree	Strongly Disagree
I feel safe in the school hallways.	Strongly Agree	Agree	Neutral	Disagree	Strongly Disagree
I feel safe in the school bathrooms.	Strongly Agree	Agree	Neutral	Disagree	Strongly Disagree
I feel safe in the classrooms.	Strongly Agree	Agree	Neutral	Disagree	Strongly Disagree

I feel safe at the school playground and/or athletic facilities.	Strongly Agree	Agree	Neutral	Disagree	Strongly Disagree
I feel safe going to and from school.	Strongly Agree	Agree	Neutral	Disagree	Strongly Disagree
Troublemakers should be suspended or expelled.	Strongly Agree	Agree	Neutral	Disagree	Strongly Disagree
Students don't get away with too much.	Strongly Agree	Agree	Neutral	Disagree	Strongly Disagree
Students know what behavior is expected of them.	Strongly Agree	Agree	Neutral	Disagree	Strongly Disagree
Teachers enforce the rules when something bad happens.	Strongly Agree	Agree	Neutral	Disagree	Strongly Disagree
Teachers listen to me when I have a problem.	Strongly Agree	Agree	Neutral	Disagree	Strongly Disagree
I can depend on my teachers to keep my school safe.	Strongly Agree	Agree	Neutral	Disagree	Strongly Disagree
Teachers enjoy teaching here.	Strongly Agree	Agree	Neutral	Disagree	Strongly Disagree
The rules for punishing students are fair.	Strongly Agree	Agree	Neutral	Disagree	Strongly Disagree
Principals apply discipline rules fairly.	Strongly Agree	Agree	Neutral	Disagree	Strongly Disagree
My school holds fire drills once per month.	Strongly Agree	Agree	Neutral	Disagree	Strongly Disagree
My school holds drills on emergencies, other than fire drills, twice per school year.	Strongly Agree	Agree	Neutral	Disagree	Strongly Disagree
My school is prepared for any emergency.	Strongly Agree	Agree	Neutral	Disagree	Strongly Disagree
My school provides guidance and counseling services I need.	Strongly Agree	Agree	Neutral	Disagree	Strongly Disagree

Other students enjoy learning.	Strongly Agree	Agree	Neutral	Disagree	Strongly Disagree
I am learning a lot in school.	Strongly Agree	Agree	Neutral	Disagree	Strongly Disagree
Doing well in school is important.	Strongly Agree	Agree	Neutral	Disagree	Strongly Disagree
My school is doing a good job.	Strongly Agree	Agree	Neutral	Disagree	Strongly Disagree
I am proud of this school.	Strongly Agree	Agree	Neutral	Disagree	Strongly Disagree

During this school year, how many times have YOU experienced and/or witnessed the following problems in your school?					
Verbal threats in school	Never	One Time This Year	One Time Per Month	One Time Per Week	Daily
Physical violence in school	Never	One Time This Year	One Time Per Month	One Time Per Week	Daily
Students with weapons in school	Never	One Time This Year	One Time Per Month	One Time Per Week	Daily
Students with drugs or alcohol in school	Never	One Time This Year	One Time Per Month	One Time Per Week	Daily
Drugs sold in school	Never	One Time This Year	One Time Per Month	One Time Per Week	Daily
Teasing or bullying in school	Never	One Time This Year	One Time Per Month	One Time Per Week	Daily
Gang activity in school	Never	One Time This Year	One Time Per Month	One Time Per Week	Daily
Stealing in school	Never	One Time This Year	One Time Per Month	One Time Per Week	Daily

Vandalism of school property	Never	One Time This Year	One Time Per Month	One Time Per Week	Daily
Discrimination or bigotry at school	Never	One Time This Year	One Time Per Month	One Time Per Week	Daily
Violence in the community around the school	Never	One Time This Year	One Time Per Month	One Time Per Week	Daily
Cheating on homework or tests	Never	One Time This Year	One Time Per Month	One Time Per Week	Daily

How effective do you feel these school policies are for making your school safe?					
Suspending students who commit acts of violence	Very Effective	Somewhat Effective	Neutral	Somewhat Ineffective	Totally Ineffective
Expelling students who commit acts of violence	Very Effective	Somewhat Effective	Neutral	Somewhat Ineffective	Totally Ineffective
Putting more security devices in school	Very Effective	Somewhat Effective	Neutral	Somewhat Ineffective	Totally Ineffective
Having more school resource officers and/or police in school	Very Effective	Somewhat Effective	Neutral	Somewhat Ineffective	Totally Ineffective
Bringing drug- and/or weapon-sniffing dogs to school	Very Effective	Somewhat Effective	Neutral	Somewhat Ineffective	Totally Ineffective
Training students in anger management and conflict resolution	Very Effective	Somewhat Effective	Neutral	Somewhat Ineffective	Totally Ineffective
Training teachers in conflict resolution	Very Effective	Somewhat Effective	Neutral	Somewhat Ineffective	Totally Ineffective
Training students to accept differences in others	Very Effective	Somewhat Effective	Neutral	Somewhat Ineffective	Totally Ineffective

Keeping drugs out of school	Very Effective	Somewhat Effective	Neutral	Somewhat Ineffective	Totally Ineffective
Having counselors to help students	Very Effective	Somewhat Effective	Neutral	Somewhat Ineffective	Totally Ineffective
Keeping weapons out of school	Very Effective	Somewhat Effective	Neutral	Somewhat Ineffective	Totally Ineffective
Involving parents more with the school	Very Effective	Somewhat Effective	Neutral	Somewhat Ineffective	Totally Ineffective
Leadership training for students	Very Effective	Somewhat Effective	Neutral	Somewhat Ineffective	Totally Ineffective

Overall I rate my school as:	The Best	Pretty Good	Neutral	Poor	The Worst

Comments:

Please list any general concerns about the safety of your school. If there is any time or place where you do not feel safe in or around the school, please describe it. We also welcome any suggestions you have to make our school safer.

Staff Survey

What is the name of your school?	
Are you male or female?	
How long have you been at this school?	
What is your role (teacher, administrator, paraprofessional, bus driver, custodian, building engineer, lunchroom worker, office staff, other)?	

Please circle the answer that most applies to YOUR experiences this school year.					
My school is generally clean.	Strongly Agree	Agree	Neutral	Disagree	Strongly Disagree
Arguments among students in school are rare.	Strongly Agree	Agree	Neutral	Disagree	Strongly Disagree
Fights among students are rare at school.	Strongly Agree	Agree	Neutral	Disagree	Strongly Disagree
Threats by students against one another are rare.	Strongly Agree	Agree	Neutral	Disagree	Strongly Disagree
Students are rarely beaten up by other students.	Strongly Agree	Agree	Neutral	Disagree	Strongly Disagree
Students are rarely picked on, called names, or teased by other students.	Strongly Agree	Agree	Neutral	Disagree	Strongly Disagree
Robbery/theft of school and personal property are rare at school.	Strongly Agree	Agree	Neutral	Disagree	Strongly Disagree
I generally feel safe at school.	Strongly Agree	Agree	Neutral	Disagree	Strongly Disagree
I feel safe on school grounds before school.	Strongly Agree	Agree	Neutral	Disagree	Strongly Disagree

I feel safe on school grounds after school.	Strongly Agree	Agree	Neutral	Disagree	Strongly Disagree
I feel safe in the school lunchroom.	Strongly Agree	Agree	Neutral	Disagree	Strongly Disagree
I feel safe in the school hallways.	Strongly Agree	Agree	Neutral	Disagree	Strongly Disagree
I feel safe in the school bathrooms.	Strongly Agree	Agree	Neutral	Disagree	Strongly Disagree
I feel safe in classrooms.	Strongly Agree	Agree	Neutral	Disagree	Strongly Disagree
I feel safe at the school playground and/or athletic fields and facilities.	Strongly Agree	Agree	Neutral	Disagree	Strongly Disagree
I feel safe going to and from school.	Strongly Agree	Agree	Neutral	Disagree	Strongly Disagree
Students don't get away with too much.	Strongly Agree	Agree	Neutral	Disagree	Strongly Disagree
Students know what behavior is expected of them.	Strongly Agree	Agree	Neutral	Disagree	Strongly Disagree
Staff enforce the rules when there is an incident.	Strongly Agree	Agree	Neutral	Disagree	Strongly Disagree
Staff monitor hallways during passing time.	Strongly Agree	Agree	Neutral	Disagree	Strongly Disagree
The rules for punishing students are fair.	Strongly Agree	Agree	Neutral	Disagree	Strongly Disagree
Students feel comfortable telling a staff person about potential violence.	Strongly Agree	Agree	Neutral	Disagree	Strongly Disagree
Teachers listen to students when they have a problem.	Strongly Agree	Agree	Neutral	Disagree	Strongly Disagree
Principals apply discipline rules fairly.	Strongly Agree	Agree	Neutral	Disagree	Strongly Disagree
My school holds fire drills once per month.	Strongly Agree	Agree	Neutral	Disagree	Strongly Disagree

My school holds drills on emergencies, other than fire drills, twice per school year.	Strongly Agree	Agree	Neutral	Disagree	Strongly Disagree
My school is prepared for any emergency.	Strongly Agree	Agree	Neutral	Disagree	Strongly Disagree
My school provides guidance and counseling services students need.	Strongly Agree	Agree	Neutral	Disagree	Strongly Disagree
Parents are involved in activities at school.	Strongly Agree	Agree	Neutral	Disagree	Strongly Disagree
Students are learning a lot in school.	Strongly Agree	Agree	Neutral	Disagree	Strongly Disagree
Staff has input into decision-making at my school.	Strongly Agree	Agree	Neutral	Disagree	Strongly Disagree
Most students are getting a good education at this school.	Strongly Agree	Agree	Neutral	Disagree	Strongly Disagree
Teachers respect students in this school.	Strongly Agree	Agree	Neutral	Disagree	Strongly Disagree
Teachers enjoy teaching here.	Strongly Agree	Agree	Neutral	Disagree	Strongly Disagree
I feel I belong at this school.	Strongly Agree	Agree	Neutral	Disagree	Strongly Disagree
Most students are proud of this school.	Strongly Agree	Agree	Neutral	Disagree	Strongly Disagree
I am proud of this school.	Strongly Agree	Agree	Neutral	Disagree	Strongly Disagree

During this school year, how many times have YOU experienced and/or witnessed the following problems in your school?					
Verbal threats on school grounds	Never	One Time This Year	One Time Per Month	One Time Per Week	Daily
Physical violence on school grounds	Never	One Time This Year	One Time Per Month	One Time Per Week	Daily
Students with weapons on school grounds	Never	One Time This Year	One Time Per Month	One Time Per Week	Daily
Students smoking on school grounds	Never	One Time This Year	One Time Per Month	One Time Per Week	Daily
Students with drugs or alcohol on school grounds	Never	One Time This Year	One Time Per Month	One Time Per Week	Daily
Drugs sold on school grounds	Never	One Time This Year	One Time Per Month	One Time Per Week	Daily
Teasing or bullying on school grounds	Never	One Time This Year	One Time Per Month	One Time Per Week	Daily
Gang activity on school grounds	Never	One Time This Year	One Time Per Month	One Time Per Week	Daily
Stealing on school grounds	Never	One Time This Year	One Time Per Month	One Time Per Week	Daily
Vandalism of school property	Never	One Time This Year	One Time Per Month	One Time Per Week	Daily
Discrimination or bigotry at school	Never	One Time This Year	One Time Per Month	One Time Per Week	Daily
Violence in the community around the school	Never	One Time This Year	One Time Per Month	One Time Per Week	Daily
Cheating on homework or tests	Never	One Time This Year	One Time Per Month	One Time Per Week	Daily
Students cutting classes and truancy	Never	One Time This Year	One Time Per Month	One Time Per Week	Daily

How effective do you feel these strategies are for making your school safe?					
Suspending students who commit acts of violence	Very Effective	Somewhat Effective	Neutral	Somewhat Ineffective	Totally Ineffective
Expelling students who commit acts of violence	Very Effective	Somewhat Effective	Neutral	Somewhat Ineffective	Totally Ineffective
Putting more security devices in school	Very Effective	Somewhat Effective	Neutral	Somewhat Ineffective	Totally Ineffective
Having more school resource officers and/or police in school	Very Effective	Somewhat Effective	Neutral	Somewhat Ineffective	Totally Ineffective
Bringing drug- and/or weapon-sniffing dogs to school	Very Effective	Somewhat Effective	Neutral	Somewhat Ineffective	Totally Ineffective
Training students in anger management and conflict resolution	Very Effective	Somewhat Effective	Neutral	Somewhat Ineffective	Totally Ineffective
Training teachers in conflict resolution	Very Effective	Somewhat Effective	Neutral	Somewhat Ineffective	Totally Ineffective
Training students to accept differences in others	Very Effective	Somewhat Effective	Neutral	Somewhat Ineffective	Totally Ineffective
Keeping drugs out of school	Very Effective	Somewhat Effective	Neutral	Somewhat Ineffective	Totally Ineffective
Having counselors to help students	Very Effective	Somewhat Effective	Neutral	Somewhat Ineffective	Totally Ineffective
Keeping weapons out of school	Very Effective	Somewhat Effective	Neutral	Somewhat Ineffective	Totally Ineffective
Involving parents more with the school	Very Effective	Somewhat Effective	Neutral	Somewhat Ineffective	Totally Ineffective
Leadership training for students	Very Effective	Somewhat Effective	Neutral	Somewhat Ineffective	Totally Ineffective

Overall I rate my school as:	The Best	Pretty Good	Neutral	Poor	The Worst

Comments:

Please list any general concerns about the safety of your school. If there is any time or place where you do not feel safe in or around the school, please describe it. We also welcome any suggestions you have to make our school safer.

Parent Survey

What is the name of your child's school?	
How many children do you have attending this school?	
What grade is your oldest child in?	
Relationship to child:	
How long has your oldest child been at this school?	
How does your oldest child typically get to school?	

Please circle the answer that most applies to YOUR OLDEST CHILD'S experiences this school year.					
My child's school is generally clean.	Strongly Agree	Agree	Neutral	Disagree	Strongly Disagree
My child has friends at this school.	Strongly Agree	Agree	Neutral	Disagree	Strongly Disagree
Arguments among students in school are rare.	Strongly Agree	Agree	Neutral	Disagree	Strongly Disagree
Fights among students are rare at school.	Strongly Agree	Agree	Neutral	Disagree	Strongly Disagree
Threats by students against one another are rare.	Strongly Agree	Agree	Neutral	Disagree	Strongly Disagree
Students are rarely beaten up by other students.	Strongly Agree	Agree	Neutral	Disagree	Strongly Disagree
Students rarely pick on, call names, or tease other students.	Strongly Agree	Agree	Neutral	Disagree	Strongly Disagree
My child has not had anything stolen at school this year.	Strongly Agree	Agree	Neutral	Disagree	Strongly Disagree
My child generally feels safe at school.	Strongly Agree	Agree	Neutral	Disagree	Strongly Disagree
My child feels safe on school grounds before school.	Strongly Agree	Agree	Neutral	Disagree	Strongly Disagree
My child feels safe on school grounds after school.	Strongly Agree	Agree	Neutral	Disagree	Strongly Disagree
My child feels safe in the school lunchroom.	Strongly Agree	Agree	Neutral	Disagree	Strongly Disagree
My child feels safe in the school hallways.	Strongly Agree	Agree	Neutral	Disagree	Strongly Disagree
My child feels safe in the school bathrooms.	Strongly Agree	Agree	Neutral	Disagree	Strongly Disagree
My child feels safe in the classrooms.	Strongly Agree	Agree	Neutral	Disagree	Strongly Disagree

My child feels safe at the school playground and/or athletic facilities.	Strongly Agree	Agree	Neutral	Disagree	Strongly Disagree
My child feels safe going to and from school.	Strongly Agree	Agree	Neutral	Disagree	Strongly Disagree
My child behaves well in school.	Strongly Agree	Agree	Neutral	Disagree	Strongly Disagree
Students don't get away with too much.	Strongly Agree	Agree	Neutral	Disagree	Strongly Disagree
My child knows the school rules.	Strongly Agree	Agree	Neutral	Disagree	Strongly Disagree
Teachers enforce the school rules.	Strongly Agree	Agree	Neutral	Disagree	Strongly Disagree
Teachers listen to my child when there is a problem.	Strongly Agree	Agree	Neutral	Disagree	Strongly Disagree
The rules for punishing students are applied fairly.	Strongly Agree	Agree	Neutral	Disagree	Strongly Disagree
This school holds fire drills once per month.	Strongly Agree	Agree	Neutral	Disagree	Strongly Disagree
This school holds drills on emergencies, other than fire drills, twice per school year.	Strongly Agree	Agree	Neutral	Disagree	Strongly Disagree
This school is prepared for any emergency.	Strongly Agree	Agree	Neutral	Disagree	Strongly Disagree
This school provides guidance and counseling services my child needs.	Strongly Agree	Agree	Neutral	Disagree	Strongly Disagree
The school regularly meets with parents.	Strongly Agree	Agree	Neutral	Disagree	Strongly Disagree
I feel welcome at the school.	Strongly Agree	Agree	Neutral	Disagree	Strongly Disagree
I can share problems I observe with teachers and administrators.	Strongly Agree	Agree	Neutral	Disagree	Strongly Disagree

My child is learning a lot in school.	Strongly Agree	Agree	Neutral	Disagree	Strongly Disagree
Overall I think this is a safe school.	Strongly Agree	Agree	Neutral	Disagree	Strongly Disagree
This school is doing a good job.	Strongly Agree	Agree	Neutral	Disagree	Strongly Disagree
I am proud of this school.	Strongly Agree	Agree	Neutral	Disagree	Strongly Disagree

During this school year, how many times has YOUR OLDEST CHILD experienced and/or witnessed the following problems in your school?

Verbal threats in school	Never	One Time This Year	One Time Per Month	One Time Per Week	Daily
Physical violence in school	Never	One Time This Year	One Time Per Month	One Time Per Week	Daily
Students with weapons in school	Never	One Time This Year	One Time Per Month	One Time Per Week	Daily
Students with drugs or alcohol in school	Never	One Time This Year	One Time Per Month	One Time Per Week	Daily
Drugs sold in school	Never	One Time This Year	One Time Per Month	One Time Per Week	Daily
Teasing or bullying in school	Never	One Time This Year	One Time Per Month	One Time Per Week	Daily
Gang activity in school	Never	One Time This Year	One Time Per Month	One Time Per Week	Daily
Stealing in school	Never	One Time This Year	One Time Per Month	One Time Per Week	Daily
Vandalism of school property	Never	One Time This Year	One Time Per Month	One Time Per Week	Daily
Discrimination or bigotry at school	Never	One Time This Year	One Time Per Month	One Time Per Week	Daily

Violence in the community around the school	Never	One Time This Year	One Time Per Month	One Time Per Week	Daily
Cheating on homework or tests	Never	One Time This Year	One Time Per Month	One Time Per Week	Daily

How effective do you feel these strategies are for making your school safe?					
Suspending students who commit acts of violence	Very Effective	Somewhat Effective	Neutral	Somewhat Ineffective	Totally Ineffective
Expelling students who commit acts of violence	Very Effective	Somewhat Effective	Neutral	Somewhat Ineffective	Totally Ineffective
Putting more security devices in school	Very Effective	Somewhat Effective	Neutral	Somewhat Ineffective	Totally Ineffective
Having more school resource officers and/or police in school	Very Effective	Somewhat Effective	Neutral	Somewhat Ineffective	Totally Ineffective
Bringing drug- and/or weapon-sniffing dogs to school	Very Effective	Somewhat Effective	Neutral	Somewhat Ineffective	Totally Ineffective
Training students in anger management and conflict resolution	Very Effective	Somewhat Effective	Neutral	Somewhat Ineffective	Totally Ineffective
Training teachers in conflict resolution	Very Effective	Somewhat Effective	Neutral	Somewhat Ineffective	Totally Ineffective
Training students to accept differences in others	Very Effective	Somewhat Effective	Neutral	Somewhat Ineffective	Totally Ineffective
Keeping drugs out of school	Very Effective	Somewhat Effective	Neutral	Somewhat Ineffective	Totally Ineffective

Having counselors to help students	Very Effective	Somewhat Effective	Neutral	Somewhat Ineffective	Totally Ineffective
Keeping weapons out of school	Very Effective	Somewhat Effective	Neutral	Somewhat Ineffective	Totally Ineffective
Involving parents more with the school	Very Effective	Somewhat Effective	Neutral	Somewhat Ineffective	Totally Ineffective
Leadership training for students	Very Effective	Somewhat Effective	Neutral	Somewhat Ineffective	Totally Ineffective

Overall I rate my school as:	The Best	Pretty Good	Neutral	Poor	The Worst

Comments:

Please list any general concerns about the safety of your child's school. If there is any time or place where you or they do not feel safe in or around the school, please describe it. We also welcome any suggestions you have to make our school safer.

Compartmentalization mapping for
proper supervision of students

When I was a student at Central High School, I left campus almost every day for four years to buy my lunch at a convenience store one block from campus. Even though the store was in a high crime area, I felt safer doing that than I did trying to eat in the poorly supervised cafeteria. When I was appointed chief of police for the school district years later, I was shocked to learn that while I was a student at the school, there had been a policy stating that students could not leave campus during the school day without permission. I had done so more than 600 times without ever getting in trouble and without even knowing that I was violating a school policy!

As a school district police chief and working with school districts across the nation, I have found students (and others) will follow rules far more often when they are clearly notified what the rules are and what the consequences of violating them are. While it seems like basic common sense, school officials sometimes forget how important it is to do this or assume they have properly notified people of policies when they in fact have not done so adequately.

In addition, I have seen many schools where students are given very little guidance as to where they can congregate on or near campus before, during and after school hours. I have visited high schools where students could gather in any unoccupied space inside or outside of the building without restriction. I have also visited high schools where hundreds of students are allowed to enter the building when the only staff member on campus is a single custodian. Both of these situations are prone to result in serious safety incidents sooner or later.

Another common problem is a failure to recognize the proper span of supervision possible for specific staff members and students during the day. For example, one elementary school we visited during recess allowed several hundred students to spread out over a large play area consisting of several acres. We observed numerous groups of children who were more than 100 yards from the nearest staff member, while at the same time we observed an adult walking a dog within twenty feet of one of these groups of students. This type of situation would make it possible for a child molester to easily lure a child away from the school. These situations make it impossible for a teacher to quickly break up a fight or render aid to a student having an asthma attack. Teachers also won't hear the words and spot the body language that can help them to identify bullying behaviors.

We suggest that school administrators carefully evaluate these issues for their campus and ensure that staff members are properly deployed in close proximity to students they are supervising in the morning, during class changes, recess, lunch and during dismissal. School officials in Helena, Montana, enhance these efforts by furnishing brightly colored vests to staff who are supervising students outside during these times. We applaud their efforts to protect Helena's school children.

One technique we recommend for our clients is to carefully evaluate their campus and determine which areas will be off limits to students during these times. Color coded maps can then be posted in several areas inside the school to show students and staff where students are allowed to congregate.

Resources

Stop Bullying Now Program
U. S. Department of Health and Human Resources
www.stopbullyingnow.hrsa.gov

Practical Information on Crisis Planning: a Guide for Schools and Communities
U. S. Department of Education Office of Safe and Drug Free Schools
www.ed.gov/emergencyplan
Or order it free by calling: 1-877-4-ED-PUBS (1-877-433-7827)

Suggested Readings

Early Warning - Timely Response – U. S. Department of Education
Can be downloaded at:
http://www.ed.gov/about/offices/list/osers/osep/gtss.html
Or order it free by calling: 1-877-4-ED-PUBS (1-877-433-7827)

Bullying at School by Dan Olweus
Blackwell Publishers; January 1, 1993. ISBN: 0631192417

The Nature of School Bullying – A Cross National Perspective
P.K. Smith, Y. Morita, J. Junger – Tas, D. Olweus, R. Catalano and P. Slee
Publisher: Routledge; November 1, 1998. ISBN: 0415179858

Teasing and Harassment – The Frames and Scripts Approach for Teachers and Parents by John H. Hoover and Glenn W. Olsen
Publisher: NES; March 5, 2001. ISBN: 1879639823

Stop Laughing at Me by Jodee Blanco
Publisher: Adams Media Corporation; March 1, 2003.
ISBN: 1580628362

A

Abuse. *See also* Bullying;
Physical abuse; Sexual molestation; Victimization
schools suppressing reports
of, 88

Accent
having a different, 52

Access control system, 69–70

ADHD, 40

Advocates, 95–99, 112

Aggravated assault, 68, 123

Aggression
responding appropriately to, 38

American Medical Association,
61

Anti-bullying programs. *See*
Bullying prevention programs

Appearances
keeping up, 87–89

Armed assault, 69

Armed robbery, 80–81

Arrests
appropriate use of, 112

Assault
aggravated, 68, 123
armed, 69
physical, 34, 118–119, 129

Assistance
mistaking sympathy for, 65

Associated Press, xix

At-risk youth
diverting from a life of crime,
124
training caregivers to recognize, 52, 60

Athletic fields
in a tactical site survey, 141

B

Barber, Cindy, ix

Barracudas, 55–71, 78–80
left in charge of other students, 65–66

Bathrooms
common problem areas, 62
redesigned for crime prevention through environmental
design, 62–63

Battered women, 67–68

Bibb County Public School
System
influencing other school districts, 107–109

Bibb County Sheriff's
Department, 98

"Big person"
having close at hand, 45

Bouyea, Robert, x

Boy Scouts of America, 96, 98

Boys and Girls Clubs of
America, 92, 96, 122
Brenner, Bill, x
Buffalo, New York, 31
Bullies
ensuring consequences for,
118
keeping everyone safe from,
xvi
of nations, 66–67
physical, 122
psychology of, 125–126
put in charge of classrooms,
65–66
standing up to, 67–69
targets of, xv–xvi
Bullying, v, viii, 47, 63–69
an " equal-opportunity"
problem, xv
defining, 118
viewed as a health issue, 61
Bullying prevention programs,
58, 120, 122
research based, 130
seminars, xi
Bullying reduction site survey
instruments, xiii
Bus drivers
parents talking with, 129

C
Cafeterias
in a tactical site survey, 140
Campus police officers, 78, 82
unarmed and unequipped, 82
Campus Safety Journal, xvi, xix
Card access control systems,
70
Caregivers
training to recognize at-risk
youth, 52, 60
Chaos in the schools, 83, 85
Child molesters
able to lure children away
from school, 165
spotting the vulnerable, 56
Civil suits
against schools, 118, 133
Cliques, 74
Clothes
wearing different, 74
College Planning and
Management, xix
Columbine High School, 36
Community
encouraging giving back to,
111
Compartmentalization mapping
for proper supervision of
students, 164–165

Consistency, 120

Contempt for school rules, 77

Council of Leaders in Alabama Schools, xi, 122

Counseling, 33. *See also* School mental health professionals

for bullies, 125–126

Crime prevention through environmental design (CPTED), 62

rest rooms designed for, 62–63

Criminal bullying

costs to the school, 122

Criminal charges

schools facing, 120

Criminal victimization, v, 34, 87

felony-grade, 68

Criminals

bringing to justice, 124

Cultural sensitivity, 44

Culture

being of a different, 37

Custom

in a tactical site survey, 141–142

D

Dangerous schools, 78

Dantzker, M. L., x

Dawson, Hal, x

Degradation, 64

Desperation, 123

Detention facilities

worse victimization than in most schools, 128

Differences

being victimized for, 37, 56

Discipline

schools failing to enforce, 78–79

Dobson, Dr. James, 129

Domestic terrorism, 59

Dorn, Chris, viii–ix, 114

Dorn, Michael Stephen. *See* Stephen

Dothan, Alabama, 35

Dress codes, 69

Drug use and selling, 78

keeping everyone safe from, xvi

Dyslexia, 40, 124

E

Early intervention

providing for at-risk youth, 52

Educators

advice for, 117–122

as advocates, 95–99
confronting problems, 96
criticized in media, 93
overworked, 92
unfit, 119
Elementary student survey,
143–147
Emergency management personnel, vi
Enderle, Jerry, ix–x
Entry-point metal detection, 48
randomizing, 49
Exploitation
before other students, 64–69

F

Facility considerations
in a tactical site survey, 135
Falling down
most common excuse given
to explain physical abuse,
67–68
Falling grades, 77
FBI National Academy program, 112
Felony-grade criminal victimization, 68
Fights breaking out, 78, 82
The fire
back into, 51–53

Fishing lures
imitating wounded fish, 60
Friends
responsible, 127

G

Gang problems, 108, 128
Gardner, Jim, x
Georgia Emergency
Management Agency
- Office of the Governor
(GEMA), xviii
School Safety Project, xviii
Terrorism Emergency
Response and Preparedness
Division, xviii
Georgia International Law
Enforcement Exchange
Program (GILEE), xix
Georgia Office of Homeland
Security, xviii
Giving of self, 99
Good Morning America, xix
Grades
falling, 77
Guns. *See also* Armed assault;
Armed robbery
confiscating, 48
keeping everyone safe from,
xvi

student weapons violations, 49

students bringing to school, 39–40, 53, 117, 119

Gymnasiums
in a tactical site survey, 141

H

Hallways and main areas
in a tactical site survey, 139–140

Health issues
bullying viewed as, 61

Heritage High School, 36

High-risk youth. *See* At-risk youth

High school hell, 85–86

Hitler, Adolf, 66–67

Home search technique, 108

I

Incident trends
reviewing and analyzing, 130
tracking, 108

Indiana School Safety Specialists Academy, xi, 121

Innocent Targets - When Terrorism Comes to School, xiv, xix

International terrorism, 59

Interventions in bullying attacks
early, providing for at-risk youth, 52
mistaking sympathy for, 65
by older youths, 47

Israel Defense Forces, xix

Israel Police, xix

J

Jane's Consultancy, xviii

Jane's Safe Schools Planning Guide for All Hazards, xix

Jones, Martha, ix

Journal of the American Medical Association, xvi

Junior Optimist Police Program, 97

K

Knives
on school buses, 86
students bringing to school, 74, 80–81

Knowing right from wrong, 32

Kollie, Ellen, x

L

LaRue, Steve, x

Law Enforcement Training Center of Middle Georgia, 103

Learning styles
  recognizing different, xxix
Legal counsel
  parents availing themselves
  of, 129
  seeking competent, vi
Level of safety
  allowing and encouraging
  students to enhance, 48
  in Bibb County Public School
  System, 107
Level of victimization, 128
Little League, 92

M

Macon Police Department, 97,
  103
Making a difference, 107–110
Mapping. *See*
  Compartmentalization map-
  ping
Marks, Judy, x
Massachusetts Department of
  Education, xi
Massachusetts Emergency
  Management Agency, xi
McCown, Don, 105
Media centers
  in a tactical site survey, 140
Mental health professionals.

See School mental health
  professionals
Metal detection, 69
  entry-point, 48, 58
  randomization of, 49
Molestation. *See* Child molest-
  ers; Sexual molestation
Moore, Deborah, x
The Mossad, xix
Moving up, 73–75
Murder, v, 34, 37, 39, 53, 117,
  122–123. *See also* Suicide
Music
  different tastes in, 37

N

National Clearinghouse for
  Educational Facilities
  (NCEF), x
National Education Association,
  xv
National School Safety Center,
  58
Near-death experience, 69
Negative predictions, 78
"Negligent privacy," 61–62, 65,
  132
Nelson, Tom, x, xvii
Nethercott, Maria, x
The New York Times, xix

Nichols, Les, 122

North Carolina Department of Public Instruction, xi

Noschang, Mary, x

Nurses. *See* School nurses

O

Older youths
intervening in a bullying attack, 47

Olweus, Dan, 120

Opportunity for victimization
"negligent privacy" providing, 62

Oral sex
compelled, 63–69

Ostracism, 75

Outcomes, 101–105

P

Parent survey, 158–163

Parents
as advocates, 97
availing themselves of legal counsel, 129
supporting their children at all costs, 129
talking with school staff, 129
withdrawing their children from schools where they are being bullied, 129–130

Pearl High School, 36

Peer groups
supportive, linking every child in the school with, 75

Peer mediation programs, 120–121
harmful in bullying situations, 121
not appropriate in bullying situations, 120

Perceived risk, 36

Perimeters
walking during a tactical site survey, 136–137, 141

Photo tutorial
downloading, xiv

Physical abuse, 122
most common excuse used for, 67–68

Physical assault, 34, 118–119, 129

Physical disabilities, 37

Pierson, Monique, ix

Plain view search technique, 108

Playgrounds
in a tactical site survey, 141

Police officers
as advocates, 97
overworked and underpaid, 92

when to call in, 129
Police records, 68
Policy
in a tactical site survey,
141–142
Policy makers
elected and appointed, xii
Political correctness
and school image issues, 70
Practical solutions, 115–166
Practice
in a tactical site survey,
141–142
Pre-incident planning system
(PIPS), 49
Predators, 55–56
spotting vulnerable children,
56, 60
Principals
attacks on, 117
benefiting from tactical site
surveys, 133
civil suits against, 118
influence of, 45
parents talking with, 129
scorned by students and
staff alike, 82
weak, 80
Privacy
"negligent," 61–62, 65, 132

Private consultants, 121, 133
Private schools, 73
Problems with the young
uncovering, 68
Procedure
in a tactical site survey,
141–142
Psychological help, 33
Psychological scars, xv
Public safety personnel, vi

R
Racial tensions, 37
addressing, 104–105
Randomization
of metal detection, 49
Randy, 39
Readings suggested, 166
Rebellion, 77–83
Recognizing at-risk youth
training caregivers for, 52,
60
Reflections, 91–94
Religion
being of a different, 37
Research-based bullying pre-
vention programs, 130
Resource guide, xiii, 166
Respite, 43–45
Responsible friends, 127

Rest rooms
designed for crime prevention through environmental design, 62–63
students dismantling, 78–79
Richardson, Beth, ix
Right from wrong
knowing, 32
Risk management personnel, vi. *See also* At-risk youth; Perceived risk
Robbery, 34
armed, 80–81
Ryan, Caroline, x

S

Safe Havens Bullying Site Survey, xiv
Safe Havens International Inc., vi, xiii, xviii, 122, 133
website of, xix, 131
Safe school climate
creation of, vi, 91
Safety. *See also* Level of safety
universally promoting the concept of, xvi
Safety nets, 112
customizing, 37, 56–60
Safety-related challenges children face, xxix

Sample plan templates
downloading, xiv
School climate surveys, 143–163
elementary student survey, 143–147
parent survey, 158–163
secondary student survey, 147–152
staff survey, 153–158
School employees
all having supervisors, 129
influencing, 131–132
wearing brightly colored vests, 165
School facilities in tactical site surveys, 139–142
athletic fields and playgrounds, 141
cafeteria, 140
gymnasium, 141
hallways and main areas, 139–140
media center, 140
policy, procedure, custom or practice, 141–142
walking the perimeter, 141
School grounds
in a tactical site survey, 137–139

School image issues, 89, 93, 120
 political correctness and, 70
School mental health professionals
 advice for, 125–126
 getting youths to open up, 125
School nurses
 advice for, 126–127
 pressuring reluctant administrators, 127
 uncovering bullying cases, 126
School Planning and Management, xix
School records, 68
School resource officers, 57, 69
 advice for, 123–124
 parents talking with, 129
School rules
 contempt for, 77
School safety
 center for, xviii
 resources on, xix
School Safety Project, xviii
School Safety Specialist, 119
School safety zone considerations
 in a tactical site survey, 134, 136–137
School Transportation News, xix
School weapons assaults
 attempted or planned, 69
 multiple victim, 117
 preventing, 108
Schools
 armed robbery in, 80–81
 chaotic, 82–83, 85
 civil suits against, 118, 133
 dangerous, 78, 89
 dropping out of, 101
 facing criminal charges, 120
 as microcosms of a community, 34
 as potential targets of terrorists in training, 59
 as prime settings for victimization, 34, 92
 as prisons of fear, 69, 71
 students bringing guns to, 39–40
 students bringing knives to, 74, 80–81
 suppressing reports of abuse, 88
Searching students for weapons, 70

Secondary student survey, 147–152

Security cameras, 57, 69–70

Self-esteem
destroying, 65

Sexual molestation, v, 32, 34, 104–105. *See also* Child molesters
before other students, 64–69
victims of, 32, 64

Sexual preference, 37

Shooting sprees, 39–40

Silence Hurts™ Campaign, 61, 69

Site survey training programs, 121

Small people
making a big difference, 47–50

Smoking in school, 78

Snapp, Clarissa, 121

Societal conditioning
encouraging acts of extreme violence, 92

Socrates, xxvii

Staff survey, 153–158

Stalin, Joseph, 66

State school safety centers
free training and technical assistance offered by, 131

Stephen F. Austin State University, xvi

Stephen (Michael Stephen Dorn), viii, xvii, xxix, 31–34, 107
appointed Chief of Police for the Bibb Country Public School System, 107
becoming a police officer, 102
encouraged to go to college, 98
encouraged to write, 96
finishing college, 105

Stephens, Ronald, 58

Stop Teaching Our Kids to Kill- -A Call To Action Against TV, Movie & Video Game Violence, 92

Student School Climate Facility Site Survey, 130

Students
allowing and encouraging to enhance the level of safety, 48
bringing guns to school, 39–40
bringing knives to school, 74, 80–81
clarifying rules for, 164

compartmentalization mapping for proper supervision of, 164–165
in danger on the way to and from school, 53
dismantling a rest room, 78–79
left unsupervised at school, 87
searching for weapons, 70
withdrawn, 85
Suggested readings, 166
Suggestions for students, parents and educators, xiii
Suicide
victims of sexual molestation committing, 101, 117
Supervision of students
compartmentalization mapping for proper, 164–165
inadequate, 121
recognizing the proper span possible, 165
Supervisors
school employees all having, 129
Supportive peer groups
linking every child in the school with, 75

Surveillance cameras, 57, 69–70
Suspicious circumstances
willingness to question, 68
Sweden, xv
Swift, Jane, ix
Sympathy
mistaking for assistance, 65

T

Tactical site surveys, 121, 130, 132–142
benefits of conducting, 133
downloading instrument for, xiv
facility considerations, 135
internally conducted, 121
other comments/considerations, 135
perimeter and school safety zone, 136–137
school facility, 139–142
school grounds, 137–139
school safety zone considerations, 134
Training Sessions for school districts, 131
Teachers
parents talking with, 129
Teamwork, 58
Teasing, v

Terrorism, 59–60

Terrorism Emergency Response and Preparedness Division, xviii

Texas Safe and Drug-Free Schools Conference (Dallas), xii

Time to notice and listen to children
taking, 93

Today's School, xix

Tokyo Broadcasting, xix

Torment, v

Tough love, 113

Training caregivers
to recognize at-risk youth, 52, 60

Truancy, 83

Tutorial
online, 121

U

Uncovering problems
with the young, 68

Unfit educators, 119

United Press International, xix

Unreported incidents of bullying, 33, 130

U.S. Department of Education, xiii, xviii

U.S. Department of Justice, xviii

V

Vandalism, 78

Victimization. *See also* Criminal victimization
emotional trauma associated with, xv
facilitating opportunities for, 62
level of, 128
preventing, 62–63
psychological help, 33
psychological scars, xv

Victims of criminal bullying, 123
losing faith in school officials, 123
parents withdrawing from that school, 129–130
reporting situations accurately and completely, 127
seeking assistance, 127

Victims of sexual molestation
attempting to cope, 33, 91, 125
committing suicide, 101
continuing the cycle, 32
dropping out of school, 101

finally reporting the event,
87–88
finally taking up weapons, 89
not reporting the event, 33,
130
reluctant to provide all relevant details, 125
seeking out help, 112
Violence
escalating, 85
fights breaking out, 78, 82, 86
at high schools, horrible acts
of, 36
schools failing to address,
78–79
societal conditioning encouraging acts of extreme, 92
Vulnerable children
predators spotting, 56

W

Weakfish, 60, 102, 107, 110
Weakfish DVD, xiv
Weapons. *See also* Guns
carrying, 74, 128
searching students for, 70
victims taking up, 89
A welcoming environment, 50
Wounded fish
fishing lures imitating, 60

Y

YMCA, 92
Youths. *See also* At-risk youth;
Older youths
conditioned by society to
commit acts of extreme violence, 92
getting to open up, 125
making the world a more
caring place for, 111
our most precious resource,
111
paying attention to, xxvii, 93
reacting differently to similar
circumstances, 102
recognizing destructive behavior in, xxix
turning to crime, preventing,
97, 124
uncovering problems with,
68
volunteering, 93
who don't fit in, identifying,
75, 77

Heartfelt Gratitude

Stephen would like to express his gratitude to the following advocates:

His father for teaching him not to fear a hard day's work.

His mother for teaching him to "make time" not excuses.

His sister Kathy for being an incredible motivator and an incurable optimist.

His brother James for showing that a man can lose his health, his family, his material possessions, and still find happiness and meaning in life.

His brother Billy for teaching him that our lives are what we make of them, not what we are dealt along the way.

His brother John for demonstrating a fierce work ethic.

Dr. Timothy Fjordbak for helping him make sense of it all.

Dr. Martha Jones for proving to the world that even a hellhole of a school can be turned into a warm, caring, fun and effective school and for instilling in me the passion and confidence to become a writer.

Mr. Coffee for having the courage to stand up to the administration of Central High School to push for efforts to address the problems of weapons and violence in the school.

Mr. Cray for taking the time to talk to his students about life.

Mrs. Olar McCown (deceased) for raising the children of the village.

Sergeant Roger Stembridge, Macon Police Department (retired), for recognizing the importance of working with youth years before it was in vogue in the field of law enforcement.

Sergeant Brooks Peterson, Bibb County Sheriff's Department, for all of the evenings and weekends you sacrificed to show the kids you cared.

Lieutenant James Defoe, Bibb County Sheriff's Department (retired), for working with kids in the community and for your combat service for your country as a United States Marine in Vietnam.

Captain Dan Barrett, Bibb County Sheriff's Department (retired), for being such an incredible role model when you did not even know you were being watched so keenly.

Special Agent Gary Kubach, Bureau of Alcohol, Tobacco and Firearms (retired), for also being a great role model.

Mr. Bob Bell for being a model scoutmaster who exceeded the norm in a field of giants.

Bud and Rita Cooper of Chattanooga, Tennessee – Bud for what you did for our country as one of the "quiet heroes" of World War II, and both of you for being the epitome of a true Christian.

The Helm Family of Perry, Georgia, for your selfless love and for showing him the importance of family.

Chief Russell E. Bentley of the Bibb County Public School System Police Department for giving back more to your community than it ever gave to you.

Dr. Jamie Cockfield, history professor at Mercer University, for instilling in him an incurable desire to learn.

Mr. Jack Napier for teaching him how to be a proper Southern gentleman.

Dixon Aldridge for fighting to get him into college despite his poor grades.

The following Bibb County Public School System Superintendents who were willing to "make waves" to work toward safer schools:
Dr. Thomas Hagler
Dr. Thomas Madision (deceased)
Dr. Gene Buinger

The following elected Bibb County Public School System Board members who showed a particular commitment to safe schools:
Mrs. Susan Cable (who later became a Georgia State Senator)
Mrs. Judy Townsend
Mrs. Betty Phillips
Mr. Don Hadaway (deceased)

And warmest regards and utmost encouragement to all of the fierce advocates for the children whom I have not yet had the pleasure and honor to meet. Keep up the good work. The children are worth it.

Help us share the powerful message you just read. *Weakfish* can be ordered online from *www.weakfish.org*

Excellent quantity pricing available, contact us for authorized distributors.

For more information on the powerful, live presentation of *Weakfish – Bullying Through the Eyes of a Child* by Michael Dorn, please email mike@weakfish.org
or visit our website at: *www.Weakfish.org*